TWAYNE'S WORLD AUTHORS SERIES

A Survey of the World's Literature

Charles Moser, George Washington University
EDITOR

RUSSIA

Valentin Kataev

TWAS 581

Valentin Kataev

VALENTIN KATAEV

By ROBERT RUSSELL
University of Sheffield

TWAYNE PUBLISHERS
A DIVISION OF G. K. HALL & CO., BOSTON

Library of Congress Cataloging in Publication Data

Russell, Robert, Ph.D.
Valentin Kataev.

(Twayne's world authors series ; TWAS 581 : Russia)
Bibliography: p.163–65
Includes index.
1. Kataev, Valentin Petrovich, 1897– Criticism and interpreta-
tion.
PG3476.K4Z79   891.73'42   80–19107
ISBN 0–8057–6423–2

To the memory of
IAN HILSON

Contents

About the Author

Robert Russell was born in Edinburgh and took both his first degree and Ph.D. at the University of Edinburgh. He teaches Russian language and literature at the University of Sheffield. His main interest is in Soviet prose, and in addition to Kataev he has published on Olesha and Zamyatin.

Preface

Valentin Kataev, now in his eighties, is one of the last survivors of a generation of Soviet writers that included such famous figures as Boris Pasternak, Vladimir Mayakovsky, Isaac Babel, and Mikhail Bulgakov. Although not, perhaps, in the first rank of Soviet writers along with those named, Kataev's contribution to Russian literature of the past sixty years has nevertheless been considerable, both in terms of the number of books he has written and in the quality of his best works. From the 1920s onwards Kataev has produced stories and longer prose works which have been typical of their age, and critics—even the most hostile—have almost all concurred in their view of him as a master of the Russian language.

Thus far no monograph and very few articles about Kataev's work have been published in the West, although he has been the subject of several doctoral dissertations in the United States and Great Britain. Of the handful of book-length studies in Russian, the most recent (Lyudmila Skorino's valuable book) was published in 1965, and so they all lack chapters on Kataev's interesting later period, which began in the mid-1960s. The present book presents an overall picture of Kataev's career from its early stages before the Revolution up to the 1970s.

Inevitably, given the constraints on length, certain omissions have proved necessary and certain other parts of Kataev's story have had to be told very briefly. Like most Soviet writers, Kataev has been reluctant to disclose details of his personal life in interviews, and so it seemed inappropriate to devote much space to biography. In the first chapter only such details of Kataev's life and times are given as are necessary to enable the reader to place his works in context.

Kataev has written in many genres—poetry and drama as well as prose—but it is as a prose writer that his contribution to Soviet literature has been greatest, and this study concentrates almost exclusively on his prose. Of his plays, only *Squaring the Circle* is discussed here. This exception has been made because *Squaring the Circle* is Kataev's best play, one which has been performed in many countries and which is still occasionally revived. Moreover, its themes and manner are those of many prose works of the 1920s, and so it may be considered as an integral part of the mainstream of Kataev's work.

I have adopted a chronological approach in this study because in this way one can readily see the parallel development of Kataev's career on the one hand and Soviet literature in general on the other. Perhaps more than any other Soviet author, Kataev has adapted his work to the particular demands and fashions of the era. The only major exception to the chronological approach occurs in the chapters devoted to the 1920s, during which period Kataev's work developed along two lines which, for the most part, remained quite separate— the one lyrical and the other satirical. These have been kept separate and are discussed in Chapters 2 and 3 respectively.

Kataev's role in Soviet literary affairs during the last twenty years or so has recently been discussed by several emigre writers. Their comments range from the highly critical to the sympathetic, and the reader who wishes to pursue this further is referred to Olga Ivinskaya's *A Captive of Time* (London: Collins, 1978), Efim Etkind's *Notes of a Non-Conspirator* (London etc.: Oxford University Press, 1978), and Anatoly Gladilin's *The Making and Unmaking of a Soviet Writer* (Ann Arbor: Ardis, 1979).

The fullest edition of Kataev's works up to 1969 is the second Collected Works, *Sobranie sochinenii v deviati tomakh* (Moscow, 1968–72). References in brackets within the text are to this edition.

ROBERT RUSSELL

University of Sheffield

Chronology

1897 Valentin Kataev born in Odessa on January 16/28.

1902 30 November/13 December. Birth of Kataev's brother, Evgeny, later famous as the writer Evgeny Petrov. Several months later Kataev's mother dies.

1910 First poem published in an Odessa newspaper. Poems published regularly in Odessa newspapers until the Civil War. Goes on extended tour of Europe with father and brother.

1914 Introduced personally to Ivan Bunin, who takes an interest in him and becomes his literary teacher.

1915 Leaves school early to fight in World War I; he is gassed, wounded, and decorated for bravery.

1917 Recovering in hospital in Odessa when October Revolution breaks out.

1918– Fights on both sides in the Civil War. Spends at least eight
1919 months in prison, most of them in the hands of the Bolsheviks.

1919– Works as a journalist in Odessa and Kharkov. Writes short
1920 stories about Civil War which are published only after move to Moscow.

1921 Death of father. Publishes "The Gold Nib," the central character of which is based on Bunin, who had emigrated in 1920.

1922 Arrives in Moscow, finds work as a journalist.

1923 Meets Vladimir Mayakovsky. Joins staff of railway workers' newspaper *The Whistle*.

1926 Publication of *The Embezzlers*.

1928 Stage version of *The Embezzlers* at the Moscow Art Theater a failure. Opening of the very successful *Squaring the Circle* at the same theater.

1930 Severely criticized for the passive optimism of his view of life. Travels round the Soviet Union with the poet Demyan Bedny, inspecting construction sites.

1932 Publication of *Time, Forward!*, Kataev's novel about the building of an industrial complex at Magnitogorsk during the first Five Year Plan.

1936   A prolonged period of creative difficulties ends with the pub-
        lication of *Lone White Sail*. Kataev hailed as a masterly writer
        of children's books.
1937   Publication of *I, a Son of the Working People*.
1938   Elected a member of the Presidium of the Union of Soviet
        Writers.
1939   Awarded Order of Lenin for services to literature.
1941–   Works as war correspondent for *Pravda* and other newspa-
1945   pers.
1942   Kataev's brother, Evgeny Petrov, killed near Sebastopol.
1946   Awarded Stalin prize for *Son of the Regiment*.
1947   Elected to Supreme Soviet of the Russian Republic.
1949   Publication of first edition of *For the Power of the Soviets*,
        rewritten after criticism in *Pravda*.
1954   Speech at Second Congress of Soviet Writers: a declaration
        of loyalty to regime.
1955   Kataev appointed first editor of new journal *Youth*. Attracts
        many talented young writers to the journal. Resigns in 1962.
1958   Joins Communist Party.
1959   Travels to United States. A more extensive trip made in the
        winter and spring of 1963.
1960s   Makes several journeys to Western Europe, especially
        France.
1965   January: completes *The Holy Well* and offers it to the journal
        Moscow. Type set, but publication stopped at last minute.
        Work eventually published in slightly modified form in *New
        World* in May 1966.
1967   Publication of *The Grass of Oblivion*.
1969   Publication of *Kubik*.
1970s   Continues to travel abroad fairly frequently.
1972   Publication of memoirs of childhood, *A Mosaic of Life: or
        The Magic Horn of Oberon*.
1978   June: publishes *My Diamond Crown*, fictionalized memoir
        about other writers of the 1920s.

CHAPTER 1

Life and Times

I Early Years

V ALENTIN Kataev was born in Odessa on January 16/28, 1897.
Petr Vasilevich Kataev, the author's father, came from a clerical
family in Vyatka and moved to Odessa in order to attend the No-
vorossiysk University. He was a good student, taking the silver
medal in the history faculty, and was offered an opportunity to stay
on at the university, but he preferred to begin work as a schoolmaster. He was a cultured, widely read man, who did everything
in his power to instill in his sons a love of literature, especially the
nineteenth-century Russian classics.

Kataev's mother, Evgeniya Ivanovna, came from the Ukraine,
and a family with strong military traditions. Until his recent series
of memoirs, especially *Razbitaia zhizn'* (*A Mosaic of Life*,1972),
Kataev had rarely portrayed or mentioned his mother in his works,
for she died when he was only six, having contracted pulmonary
edema a few months after the birth of her second child, Evgeny.[1]
(Evgeny would eventually achieve fame as the writer Evgeny Petrov, one half of the partnership of Ilya Ilf and Evgeny Petrov, who
together wrote several very funny and popular satirical novels and
stories in the 1920s and 1930s.) After the death of his wife, Petr
Vasilevich was helped to bring up his young sons by his sister-in-
law, Elizaveta Ivanovna Bachey. That family structure would provide Kataev with a model for more than one fictional family.

At eight years of age Valentin Kataev entered the preparatory
class of one of Odessa's high schools, and within a year he had begun
writing verses. The summer of 1907 was spent in a cottage by the
sea in Bessarabia, and Kataev completed ten poems during the
family's stay there. During that same summer he first tried writing
prose, with a description of the village post office and of the moon
rising over the sea. In 1910 Petr Vasilevich and his two sons took

13

an extended holiday, visiting several European countries, an experience which provided material for part of the novel *Khutorok v stepi (The Small Farm in the Steppe)*, written over forty years later.

In the summer of 1910 Kataev met the poet Alexander Fedorov, the father of a school friend and the central figure in an Odessan literary and artistic circle. Fedorov read Kataev's poems, recognized in them a faint glimmering of talent, and introduced the young boy to the work of the famous poet and prose writer, Ivan Bunin. Four years later he arranged for Kataev to meet Bunin in person when the latter came to Odessa for the summer. It was a meeting which was to have a profound effect on Kataev, for in Bunin he found a literary master to take as a model.

Kataev's patriotic feelings, evident from some of his early verses, were inflamed by the outbreak of World War I, and he could not wait to finish school before volunteering for the army.[2] From 1915 until August 1917 he served with an artillery brigade and was concussed, gassed, and twice wounded. During his years of military service he continued to write poems and short stories, as well as brief, impressionistic war dispatches which were published in Petrograd journals and Odessa newspapers.[3] (He had published a few poems in Odessa newspapers before the war, with his first published poem appearing in 1910.)

By a stroke of good fortune Kataev was slightly wounded in the early stages of the offensive on the Rumanian front in June 1917, and was thereby spared the considerable risk of death or serious injury in the later stages of that campaign. As a wounded officer (he held the rank of ensign), he was returned to Odessa for hospital treatment, and he was in the Odessa Military Hospital when the October Revolution took place. That began three of the most complicated years of Kataev's life—the years of the Civil War.

II *The Civil War Years*

Despite the anxiety over such facts of life in the Odessa of 1918 as rampant inflation and extreme political uncertainty, the young poets of the city spent much of their time in literary pursuits and formed a society to give themselves a public forum for their work.[4] They chose the title "The Green Lamp" for their new group, thereby linking themselves with the poet Alexander Pushkin, who had taken part in a more famous "Green Lamp" literary circle about a century before. The Odessa literary club first met in September 1917, and flourished until the spring of 1919, numbering among its members several young poets, such as Eduard Bagritsky, Yury Olesha, and Kataev, who were later to become famous.

Meetings were held either in a private apartment or, when the society grew larger, in the Conservatory or University.[5] At one meeting Kataev, wearing his officer's uniform and still suffering from the effects of gas, read his "Three Love Sonnets." One member of the audience on that occasion later wrote: "Everyone instantly listened with respect, for Kataev was already well known by virtue of the many marvellous poems of his which had appeared in print."[6] "The Green Lamp" was succeeded by another literary society called "The Poets' Collective," the meetings of which Kataev also attended.[7]

At the beginning of June 1918, Bunin and his wife arrived in Odessa to escape from Soviet Russia. (The fighting had not yet reached so far South.) They remained in the city through several changes of government until January 1920. Kataev called on them soon after their arrival, renewing the friendship which had begun in 1914, and during the eighteen months or so which Bunin spent in Odessa in 1918 and 1919 Kataev was a frequent visitor at the famous writer's home. He often asked Bunin to comment on a poem or a story he had written and Bunin would do so—sometimes criticizing, but generally praising his young pupil. Vera Nikolaevna Bunina has left a picture of Kataev as he appeared to her in the summer of 1918: "I cast sidelong glances at Kataev, at his dark, slightly morose face, at his thick black hair above a firm low brow. I listened to his staccato speech with its slight southern accent. His favorite author is Tolstoy, about whom he speaks with great enthusiasm, then Chekhov, Maupassant, Flaubert, Daudet . . . He is very smart and has a good appreciation of poetry. For the moment he is very candid."[8]

But although much of Kataev's time in 1918 and 1919 was spent in writing and thinking about literature and visiting his mentor, he was also actively involved in the Civil War. To be sure, his brief autobiographical note of 1959 makes no mention of the year 1918, and of the Civil War Kataev says only: "In 1919 I was mobilized into the Red Army and served for a while as a battery commander during battles on the Lozavaya-Poltava line."[9] In his 1928 autobiography, however, he paints a more complex picture of his activity during the Civil War: "The Civil War of 1918–20 in the Ukraine left me utterly exhausted, tossing me from the Whites to the Reds, from the counter-revolution to the Cheka. In all I spent at least eight months in jail during those years."[10]

Vera Bunina's diary adds some detail to the picture of Kataev's Civil War activity. She makes it quite clear that Kataev, like many of the other young poets of Odessa, did not support the Red cause from the beginning of the Civil War, but only from the spring of 1919, when the French and English interventionists left the city and it fell to the Bolsheviks. Until a few days before the change of power in Odessa Kataev had served in the Volunteer White Army.[11] In view of the severe punishment meted out by the Reds to the White soldiers they captured—the officers were executed and the men whipped with ramrods—Kataev was fortunate to escape detection.

After his brief spell in the Red Army in 1919 Kataev worked for a while as a journalist in Odessa. "I was put in charge of the 'satire windows' at the Odessa branch of the Russian Telegraph Agency, ROSTA. . . . I wrote captions for propaganda posters, verses, slogans, leaflets. I took part in 'oral' newspapers etc."[12] One of his duties while working for the Odessa branch of ROSTA was to visit outlying villages in order to recruit some of the local inhabitants as correspondents, and while engaged in this work in 1920 he had the narrow escape from death at the hands of terrorists which he describes vividly in *Trava zabven'ia (The Grass of Oblivion)* (IX, 355–57).[13] At this time he also underwent a severe bout of typhus.

The following year Kataev moved to Kharkov, where he continued to work for ROSTA, producing verse, slogans, and a "heroic drama" which received just one performance. It was a period which he was to look back on with nostalgia as "a uniquely wonderful time," despite the fact that he often had to go hungry.[14] The editor of *Kommunist*—one of the newspapers for which he worked—was "the indomitable Sergey Ingulov," a committed Communist who constantly exhorted his young colleagues to write from a Bolshevik standpoint. It was under Ingulov's stern editorship that Kataev published a satirical portrait of Bunin in the story "Zolotoe pero" ("The

Gold Nib"). His stay in Kharkov was brief, however, for at the beginning of 1922, after the death of his father, Kataev moved to Moscow, which he had resolved "to take by storm."[15]

III   *Moscow in the 1920s*

When the turmoil of the Civil War years began to settle and the period of the New Economic Policy (NEP), which made certain concessions to private enterprise, got under way, scores of provincial journalists, poets, and authors made their way to Moscow, drawn by the prospect of national fame after the years of literary starvation. From Odessa came a number of authors who were to make an important contribution to Russian literature in the 1920s: Olesha, Bagritsky, Ilf, Petrov, Vera Inber, and Kataev, as well as many of lesser stature.[16]

For most of the aspiring young authors journalism provided a means of staying alive while they awaited the publication of their literary work. Soon after his arrival in Moscow Kataev began writing satirical sketches for the newspaper *Trud (Labor)*. At the same time he met Nadezhda Krupskaya, Lenin's wife, who invited him to write some pamphlets for the Political Education Department which she headed, and, as a result, Kataev produced a short account of the government's housing policy. A journalist who knew him well in the 1920s has written that "a careless attitude towards his talent led Kataev to waste it in many ways. He was very pleased when, at the beginning of the NEP period he wrote and published a pamphlet entitled 'The New Housing Policy.' "[17] Krupskaya introduced Kataev to the novelist Alexander Serafimovich, who was preparing to launch a journal entitled *Novy mir (New World)* and was looking for an editorial secretary. Kataev got the position and published in the journal one or two of the stories that he had brought with him from Odessa. But it was a short-lived job, for the journal ceased publication after only two issues and Kataev moved to the railway workers' newspaper *Gudok (The Whistle)*, with which he was associated for most of the 1920s.

Despite its origins as a specialized newspaper designed for a particular type of worker, *Gudok* had a wide circulation. In 1927, for example, it sold 400,000 copies daily and provided employment for some five hundred correspondents.[18] It was here, at *Gudok*, that

the younger writers who had migrated to Moscow from Odessa and
Kiev found work. Yury Olesha wrote a daily satirical verse under
the pseudonym "Zubilo" ("The Chisel"); Mikhail Bulgakov contributed short satirical sketches; Olesha and Ilf answered readers' letters
in their witty verse; Kataev wrote both verse and prose sketches
under a number of pseudonyms, including "Oliver Twist."[19]

During these years the problem of living accommodation in Moscow was particularly acute. Many of the young writers at *Gudok*
had to live in crowded dormitories or share one of the corridor-like
cells into which the large rooms of old houses were divided by
means of thin plywood partitions. In these circumstances Kataev
was indeed fortunate to have a two-room apartment on Mylnikov
Lane where those who lived in less spacious accomodation gathered
in the evenings to read and criticize each other's work.[20]

Throughout the 1920s Soviet writers constantly grouped and re-
grouped into associations, issued manifestoes, and engaged in arguments over literature and its relationship to society. The major
division was between those writers who were Communists and active supporters of the regime (Proletarians, as they were called) and
those who were not. The principal grouping of the Proletarian authors was RAPP, the Russian Association of Proletarian Writers.
Kataev never belonged to a close-knit formal group, but he was one
of the so-called fellow-travelers—the large group of writers who
gave tacit assent to the Soviet regime but who stopped short of
actively supporting it. When the Communist Party in effect declared
in 1925 its continued neutrality in the squabbles between rival
literary groups, it was possible until the last years of the decade for
fellow-travelers to write in a variety of styles on a variety of subjects
without official condemnation, and in this atmosphere of relative
freedom many fine works appeared. The spirit of the NEP period
suited Kataev's talent perfectly, and the best of his satire and drama
and some of his most notable short stories were written at this time.

Most of those who gathered at Kataev's home to read their work
were, like him, fellow-travelers, but not all of his friends belonged
to this large group. In 1923 he became acquainted with several
members of the LEF (Left Front of Art) group, notably Mayakovsky,
and he remained on friendly terms with the Futurist poet, whom
Stalin was to call "the best poet of our Soviet epoch," until his
suicide in 1930. Even before moving to Moscow, Kataev had longed
to meet Mayakovsky, whom he had heard at readings in Odessa and

Kharkov.[21] According to Kataev, he eventually met the poet by stopping him in the street and introducing himself.[22] Mayakovsky lived near Mylnikov Lane and became a frequent visitor to Kataev's apartment, as the latter recalls in *The Grass of Oblivion*. After Mayakovsky's death Kataev often recorded his debt to the great poet, who provided him with a model of a committed Soviet writer prepared to use his art to support the regime. At least in retrospect, Kataev regarded his friendship with Mayakovsky as having had a profound ideological impact on him.[23] And so, during the early part of his career, Kataev came under the influence of two great figures in Russian literature— Bunin and Mayakovsky—who were the complete antithesis of each other. Although he did not admit it in print until almost forty years later, Kataev considered himself a pupil of both Bunin and Mayakovsky. In the work produced during those forty years the influence of both masters can be seen, as can the results of attempting to reconcile two such opposite forces.

In the mid-1920s, while writing satirical sketches and poems for *Gudok*, Kataev continued to write short stories, and in 1926 he produced a short comic novel entitled *Rastratchiki (The Embezzlers)* which proved enormously successful and was published in translation in Paris, New York, London, Vienna, Budapest, Prague, Warsaw, and Madrid. Suddenly Kataev had achieved his ambition of taking Moscow by storm: *The Embezzlers* was one of the most popular Soviet works of the period. Maxim Gorky, keeping a close eye on Soviet literary events from his home in Sorrento, gave the novel his approval, and when Kataev and Leonid Leonov, the author of *Vor (The Thief)*, visited him in 1927 he greeted them with the remark "Ah, here come the thieves and the embezzlers."[24]

The Embezzlers also caught the eye of another almost legendary figure in Russian cultural life—Konstantin Stanislavsky, the Director of the Moscow Art Theater, who was looking for young Soviet dramatists to write a series of new, modern plays for the theater. In the 1926–27 season the theater introduced a successful stage version of Bulgakov's novel *The White Guard* (staged as *The Days of the Turbins*), and the following year it repeated the experiment of asking novelists to write dramatic versions of their works. Vsevolod Ivanov's *Armored Train 14–69* and Kataev's *The Embezzlers* were first produced in December 1927 and April 1928 respectively, but whereas the former proved very popular, Kataev's play was a failure and closed after only eighteen performances.[25] The experience of working in the Moscow Art Theater turned out to be both thrilling and frustrating for Kataev. (And also, incidentally, for Bulgakov, whose short novel *Teatral'nyi roman*—translated into English as *Black Snow*—gives a very good and funny picture of the difficulties a young dramatist faced in dealing with the eccentricities of some of the famous personalities of the Moscow Art Theater.) In Stanislavsky, Kataev found himself confronted by someone whose view of *The Embezzlers* differed sharply from his own. For Kataev, the play and the novel were essentially comic grotesques in which social comment was only implied, whereas Stanislavsky tried to weigh the play down with psychological motivation which it could not bear. As he was to say afterwards, "Kataev is a magnificent observer, sharp and subtle, but he is no Gogol. He does not try to elevate the world with his work."[26]

The failure of the stage version of *The Embezzlers* naturally upset Kataev, and when his next play, *Kvadratura kruga (Squaring the Circle*, 1927), was in rehearsal at the Moscow Satire Theater and the Art Theater he took care to ensure that it was not similarly misinterpreted by announcing in advance that it was a comedy which neither posed nor sought to solve any problems. *Squaring the Circle* turned out to be as much of a success as the novel *The Embezzlers* had been, running for over six hundred performances at the Moscow Art Theater, and proving popular with countless amateur dramatic societies all over the Soviet Union. Like *The Embezzlers*, it brought Kataev a certain international reputation, for it was staged in several European countries as well as in America.[27]

By the end of the 1920s Kataev's position in Soviet literature appeared settled: he was a well-known fellow-traveler capable of producing witty, stylish satirical works, lyrical short stories, and well observed cameos of life in Moscow under NEP conditions. But as the NEP period drew to a close, to be succeeded by the era of Socialist reconstruction—the first Five Year Plan—the relatively relaxed literary atmosphere of the 1920s began to give way to a much tenser one. The attacks on fellow-travelers by members of the RAPP group grew more extreme, and the Party's toleration of different shades of opinion and varying themes and styles in literature yielded to an increasing demand for uniformity and active support. For Kataev, the impending changes were heralded by a critical article written by a RAPP critic, Iosif Mashbits-Verov, published toward the end of 1930.[28] Entitled "Na grani" ("On the Brink"), it reviewed Kataev's work of the 1920s and concluded that the author was "on the brink" of being anti-Soviet. The implied threat could not but have affected Kataev, even though it came from RAPP and not directly from the Party. A change of direction was called for. Not all fellow-travelers were able to oblige; some preferred to practice what the short-story writer Isaac Babel, a few years later, called "the genre of silence."[29] But most did try to change—to lend active support to the regime in their works—and Kataev was among their number.

IV *The 1930s*

The first Five Year Plan of national development was launched in October 1928; five months later the Party decided to implement it in four years. As part of the task of encouraging people to work harder, writers and other artists were sent on visits to factories, construction sites, and model communes to observe and report on the progress being made. Writing in 1957, Kataev recalled that in October 1930 he had taken part in the "All-Union Shock Workers' Day" when a group of about eighty writers and composers had visited several Moscow factories. At the same time he had been one of a group of writers who had signed an agreement to cooperate with a particular factory, as was the custom at the beginning of the 1930s.[30]

In fact, however, as early as 1929 Kataev had made an inauspicious start to the task of providing literary support for the Five Year Plan by reporting unfavorably on his visit to the Moscow Brake Factory, undertaken in the summer of that year. The factory had entered into socialist competition with another, and it was Kataev's task to report on the effect of the competition on workers.[31] What he saw did not fulfill his expectations of "struggle, a raised temperature, a quickened pulse, a vein standing out on the forehead." Instead, there was "a scene of the most profound material well-being, contentment and even . . . inertia."[32] The workers were outraged and soon hit back by commenting to journalists that Kataev came from the middle class, had no idea what real work involved, and had written an insulting sketch based on the most superficial observation.[33]

The next month Kataev published his impressions of a visit to a model commune set up by Russians who had emigrated to the United States in tsarist times and had returned to Soviet Russia.[34] Further visits included one with a large group of other writers to the site of the White Sea Canal, which eventually led to the writing of a book by the entire group.[35]

In the early 1920s Kataev had met Demyan Bedny, a writer of propaganda verses and a political figure of some importance who lived in the Kremlin. For most of 1930 and the early part of 1931 Bedny travelled around the country's major construction sites in a private railway carriage which he, as a man of privilege, had at his disposal, and on several of these journeys he was accompanied by Kataev. The young author thus had a chance to visit the site of the Dnepr hydroelectric power station, the Rostov Agricultural Machinery Plant, the Stalingrad Tractor Factory, and, finally, the huge industrial complex at Magnitogorsk. Kataev left Bedny's train in order to stay at Magnitogorsk from May 1931 until the following spring, and then spent a few weeks in Paris writing his novel *Vremia, vpered!* *(Time, Forward!)*, which he came to look on as an important turning point in his life: "To see with one's own eyes how our country is being transformed from an agrarian land into an industrial one results in a change in one's outlook as a writer . . . The journeys I have made around our country have filled me with a feeling of incredible pride."[36]

The last of Kataev's visits to factories and collective farms took place in the summer of 1934, when he spent several months attached to the political section of an MTS (Machine Tractor Station, a unit which maintained tractors and other agricultural machinery for use on collective farms). He intended to incorporate the material which he collected into a novel on an agricultural theme which would parallel his industrial novel, but the project was never completed. The period of Kataev's direct involvement in "construction literature" was over.

In April 1932 RAPP was dissolved by a Party decree. Most of the former fellow travelers undoubtedly heaved a sigh of relief that an organization which had subjected them to so much criticism no longer existed.[37] Its semiofficial position as an intermediary between the Party and non-Party writers had led some of its members to regard themselves as arbiters of what might and might not be written. However, RAPP's dissolution did not mean a return to the freedom of the NEP period. Writers were just as constrained in their choice of theme and style as they had been in the previous two years, as can be seen by reading between the lines of a newspaper article written by Kataev on the first anniversary of RAPP's dissolution. "Formerly it was possible to blame RAPP for all one's creative and ideological faults. Now each of us is fully responsible to the Party for himself. There is no one to blame. The trust which the Party has invested in authors brings with it many responsibilities . . . Only by struggling to acquire a proper literary technique and philosophical content shall we create a literature worthy of our remarkable era."[38]

The dissolution of RAPP was soon followed by the establishment of a single Union of Soviet Writers which held its first Congress in 1934, when, in the key speeches by Gorky and Andrey Zhdanov, the notion of Socialist Realism as the basic method of Soviet art and literature was advanced. This method required writers to portray "reality in its revolutionary development": in other words, to present an idealized picture by projecting onto present-day society the changes that it was anticipated would come about in the future. Secondly, Socialist Realism laid on authors the task of "the ideological remaking and education of workers in the spirit of socialism," which amounted to a requirement to write didactically, so that readers might be inspired to emulate the heroes of works of fiction who, for example, adhered strictly to the Party line. The didactic function of Socialist Realism meant that suitable works for children and young people were particularly encouraged. Between 1931 and 1935 prominent figures in Soviet cultural and political life, such as Gorky and Krupskaya, advocated a richer and more extensive socialist literature for children.

The official encouragement of children's literature came at a time when Kataev was experiencing great creative difficulties. Several projects, including his novel about collective farming, had been abandoned.[39] When he was approached by a publishing house to write a book for children he found it a liberation from the difficulties of writing about modern industrial or agricultural life, which he knew only superficially. The mid-1930s trend toward historical novels and novels for young people suited Kataev's talent perfectly, and in 1936 he wrote *Beleet parus odinokii (Lone White Sail)*, a work based in large measure on his recollections of childhood in Odessa.[40]

In the same year Kataev began to write articles and sketches for

Pravda, and in 1937 he was asked by the editor to put aside all
other projects in order to write something that would reflect the
deterioration in Soviet-German relations. He was given access to
papers in the *Pravda* archives relating to the German occupation
of part of the Ukraine in 1918 and used them as the foundation for
Ia, syn trudovogo naroda (I, a Son of the Working People). Once
again he had adapted his work to produce a tale suitable for its
period. (Eisenstein's film *Alexander Nevsky*, which takes as its subject an earlier invasion of Russian soil by Teutonic forces, was completed in 1938, and there were several other works on similar lines
at this time.)

In 1935 Kataev married Esther Davydovna Brenner, who was
then in her early twenties, and by the end of the decade he was the
father of two children, a daughter, Evgeniya and a son, Pavel.
(There had been an earlier marriage to Anna Sergeevna Kovalenko,
which dated from 1923.)[41] He now enjoyed a degree of official approval which conferred considerable privilege and material reward.
In 1938 he became a member of the Presidium of the Writers'
Union and the following year he was awarded the Order of Lenin
for services to literature. When a new block of flats in Lavrushinsky
Lane was made available to writers, Kataev and his wife received
one and were able to fill it with modern furniture, including a
refrigerator. Nadezhda Mandelshtam, the widow of the poet Osip
Mandelshtam who died in a prison camp, recalls that "in Kataev's
new apartment everything was new—including his wife and child
and the furniture."[42] A decade that began with the threat contained
in the RAPP critic's article ended with wealth, privilege, and his
official recognition as a valuable supporter of the regime. While
others perished, Kataev adapted and survived.

V *The War and the Postwar Years*

During World War II Kataev worked for Soviet Radio and the
Information Bureau and served as a war correspondent for *Pravda*
and other newspapers.[43] His duties took him to several battle fronts,
including the Battle of Orel. His brother, Evgeny Petrov, also
served as a war correspondent, and on one of his assignments in
1942 he was killed when his plane was shot down near Sebastopol.[44]
In April 1944 Kataev visited the recently liberated Odessa and spoke
to partisans about life in the catacombs, an experience that provided

him with material for his novel *Za vlast' Sovetov* (*For the Power of the Soviets*), the first version of which appeared in 1949.

The years between the end of the war and Stalin's death were the most oppressive in the history of Soviet literature, a time when novels and plays had to present an increasingly formulaic picture of Soviet society, giving due prominence to the role of the Party as the vanguard of the people. As with the more famous case of Alexander Fadeev's *Molodaia gvardiia* (*The Young Guard*), Kataev was forced by threatening negative criticism to rewrite his only long work of these years—*For The Power of the Soviets*—to bring it into line with the very strict demands of the age. He spent a great deal of his time on this patently sterile task, and the result was no real improvement in a novel that had been weak to begin with. Thus, for Kataev as for many other writers the immediate postwar years (sometimes termed the "Zhdanov period" after Stalin's spokesman on cultural affairs, Andrey Zhdanov) proved to be lost time. But even while his creative talents stagnated, Kataev's reputation as a public figure was enhanced by the award of a Stalin prize for the tale *Syn polka* (*Son of the Regiment*), written during the war, and by his election in 1947 to the Supreme Soviet of the Russian Federation.[45]

The years following the death of Stalin saw a relaxation in Party control over the arts and the emergence of many talented young writers. "The Thaw," as this period came to be called, was heralded by an article in *Novy mir* as early as December 1953,[46] and was given a great boost by the setting up in 1955 of a new journal for young people entitled *Yunost* (*Youth*), under Kataev's editorship. Among the contributors to *Yunost* were such notable young poets and writers as Andrey Voznesensky, Vasily Aksenov, Anatoly Gladilin, and Anatoly Kuznetsov, some of whom have remained on close terms with Kataev.[47] By the time ill-health forced Kataev to resign as editor in 1962, *Yunost* had an enviable reputation and a huge circulation, and undoubtedly his energetic editorial work and ability to spot and encourage talented newcomers were major factors in its success.

One result of the Thaw was that Soviet authors began to travel abroad, and a literature that had been almost entirely insular for decades began to take account of other countries. In the 1950s and 1960s Kataev made journeys to China, the United States, and several European countries, and he has made frequent trips abroad in the last few years, often lecturing in university Slavic departments.[48] His experience of travel has formed one of the basic elements in his later works.

From the early 1930s onward Kataev frequently emphasized in speeches and articles that, although not formally a member of the Communist Party, he considered himself to be a non-Party Bolshevik, rather like Gorky.[49] In 1958 he finally joined the Party, a step which he described as "the logical conclusion of my entire spiritual life."[50] There may be some doubts about the motives that impelled Kataev to transform himself at the beginning of the 1930s from a fellow-traveler into an active supporter of the regime, but of the sincerity of his conviction in recent years there can be no question. He is now, in his old age, a member of the Communist Party who believes fully in that Party's policies, and for whom the concept of his native land has become almost inseparable from that of the Party. Yet his work retains elements that recall the carefree fellow-traveler of the 1920s and that are, to some extent, in conflict with his public expressions of support for the Party. Much of his later work has been an attempt to reconcile these two elements.[51]

At the time of this writing, Kataev lives with his wife in the village of Peredelkino, near Moscow, where many writers have their homes. He has retained his Moscow apartment, but rarely stays there, preferring the countryside to the city. Although still formally a member of the Presidium of the Writers' Union, he now takes little part in the activities of that body. But he is in no sense in retirement. A constant flow of works since the mid-1960s—notably *Sviatoi kolodets* (*The Holy Well,* 1966) and *The Grass of Oblivion,* both of which engendered some controversy and led the critics to speak of a "new" Kataev—attests to his great vigor and abiding literary ambition. Moreover, the high quality of some of these works has given his career a new dimension at a time when most of his surviving contemporaries have ceased writing. He is now almost the last representative of his generation—the first generation of Soviet authors—to be actively writing. And although several of his recent works have been of the one type, his surprising capacity for self-renewal means that it is impossible to predict what his next work will be like. In his eighties he still has the ability to astonish and sometimes delight his readers.

CHAPTER 2

The Fellow-Traveler: Short Stories

I Early Poetry

KATAEV's reputation rests on his prose work and, to a lesser degree, on the best of his plays, such as *Squaring the Circle*, but he began his career as a poet and has reverted to poetry at various times throughout his life. Much of his very early verse is typically adolescent in its themes (mostly religious and patriotic) and its generalized emotion.[1] Many years later Kataev commented that before he became acquainted with Bunin's work he believed that poetry could only be written on certain themes and that the secret of being a poet lay in collecting together all possible rhymes.

After his introduction to Bunin, Kataev began to imitate certain features of the older poet's style, and soon the quality of his verse improved as he gradually rejected generalized emotion expressed in "poetic" language in favor of an increasing awareness of the specific quality of material objects. Looking back on this period of his life in *The Grass of Oblivion*, he recalled the shock that accompanied his realization that Bunin's poetry was about everyday experiences; that in a Bunin poem about the sea and a seagull he could recognize the place being described, and through Bunin's comparison of a floating seagull and a fisherman's float bobbing on the surface he had his eyes opened to a phenomenon that he had seen many times but never grasped.[2] "I saw the miracle of real poetry: a new world opened up before me" (IX, 264).

Kataev's own poetry never reached the standard set by Bunin, but in the best of his early poems, such as "Sukhovei" ("Hot Dry Wind") and "Znoi" ("Heat") (both 1915), and "Kassiopeia" ("Cassiopeia," 1918) he at least shows himself a worthy pupil.[3] These poems attempt to convey as accurately as possible a moment when the poet's senses were acutely attuned to the sights, sounds, and smells around him. The merit of Kataev's poetry lies in the precision with which he conveys physical sensations. Though some of his verses are insignificant, he does occasionally reveal in them the qualities of sensuous receptivity and accuracy of description that distinguish much of his mature lyrical prose.

II *Early Stories*

Some of Kataev's best short stories date from the 1920s, but in the previous decade he had written a few that indicated where his strength would lie once he matured. His lifelong interest in children and adolescents first emerges in such stories as "Ruzh'e" ("The Gun," 1915), "Vesennii zvon" ("Spring Chimes," 1916) and "Sviatki u pokoinikov" ("Yuletide at Pokoy," 1918).[4] Five-year-old Shurka Perchenko, the hero of "The Gun," is the first in a long line of children in Kataev's work who discover that wealth brings fame and prestige. In Shurka's case wealth takes the form of a German gun, given to him by his father. He almost succumbs to the temptation to sell it for a "weighty silver ruble which produced a ringing sound" (I, 68), but soon realizes that his rifle is worth much more than a ruble to him because of the envy and admiration which it inspires among his friends. With such a desirable possession he finds himself in a position of power, able to grant or withhold permission to touch the treasured weapon as his whim dictates. The theme of wealth and the power which accompanies it recurs in so many of Kataev's works that it must be recognized as one of his major preoccupations. Time after time he returns to the psychology of a person, especially a child, who desperately wishes to be rich.

"Spring Chimes" and "Yuletide at Pokoy" are both autobiographical stories. The former deals with adolescent love. Its hero is a twelve-year-old boy who reads Romantic literature and imagines that he is in love with a girl called Tanya. In fact, he knows very little about Tanya, who merely enables him to manufacture the sweet, self-indulgent melancholy that he enjoys. The boy does whatever he can to sustain his highly emotional state. Jealousy, guilt, and pride are feelings to be nourished and savored. While the author identifies and sympathizes with his adolescent hero, he does not allow him to escape his ironical glance, and the warm humor of the story derives from the author's finely modulated, gentle irony.

A similar tone pervades "Yuletide at Pokoy," in which the same boy, a little older this time, indulges himself by staging a play for the Christmas entertainment of his family and friends. Many details of the boy's home and family correspond to what is known of Kataev's early life. Like Kataev, the boy's name is Valentin; his brother, Zhenya, is a dark-haired child with round, protruding ears and a lolling tongue; his father resembles the writer Anton Chekhov. As in "Spring Chimes," the hero lives in a constant state of exaggerated emotion, imagining himself to be a nineteenth-century Romantic literary hero such as Pushkin's Onegin, or Chatsky, the central figure of Alexander Griboedov's play *Gore ot uma (Woe from Wit)*.

Both "Spring Chimes" and "Yuletide at Pokoy" exhibit some of the features that were to distinguish Kataev's mature prose: his ear for children's dialogue, his warmly ironical attitude to autobiographical heroes, his limpid, lyrical descriptive passages. Perhaps the most interesting feature of both stories is the point of view, which shifts between the author and his character, a more youthful version of himself. This mode of narration is achieved by alternating between a vocabulary and intonation characteristic of a young boy and a more adult style: the author both identifies with his autobiographical character and simultaneously keeps him at a certain distance through irony. This tone would become characteristic of many subsequent works.

A more somber tone prevails in "Zemliaki" ("Fellow Countrymen," 1916) and "Noch'iu" ("At Night," 1917), two stories reflecting Kataev's experience in World War I. "Fellow Countrymen" is set in a temporary field hospital. Three wounded men lie listening while a fourth patient, suffering from venereal disease, boasts of his sexual conquest of grass widows. Later it transpires that one of the listeners is the husband of a woman seduced by the storyteller. In this brief story Kataev manages to convey an atmosphere of boredom, sickness, and despair which enters into a contradiction with the potentially melodramatic narrative. The most notable feature of "Fellow Countrymen" is the use of colloquial language by the peasant soldiers, especially the boastful central character whose speech reveals him as a shallow, ignorant egotist. In its use of colloquial direct speech "Fellow Countrymen" bears a superficial resemblance to Mikhail Zoshchenko's short stories, but there is no humor in Kataev's tale, and the speech is less stylized than that of Zoshchenko's characters.

"At Night"—written in 1917 but suppressed by the Provisional Government censorship because of its pessimistic tone and published only in 1934—bears witness to Kataev's growing maturity. His war journalism—such sketches as "This is the Way a Russian Soldier Dies" and "Soldiers Learn to Write"—had shown him to be a compassionate observer, interested more in soldiers' routine activities, such as playing checkers or making spoons out of shrapnel, than in describing battles and victories.[5] The domestic note struck in the majority of the sketches contrasts with the chauvinistic tone of many of Kataev's poems written during the first year of the war, and indicates a changing view of the nature of war.[6] "At Night" confirms this change. The main protagonists are not heroic defenders of Russia, or even the quiet, dignified men of a sketch like "This is the Way a Russian Soldier Dies." They are lost, confused, and frightened soldiers wandering blindly in search of their unit and terrified lest they meet an enemy patrol. The narrator is tormented by memories of his happy pre-war life, when he ate ice cream, went fishing, played tennis, and listened to Tchaikovsky's *1812 Overture* at a symphony concert. In his memory the strong, beautiful notes take on colors and textures which delight him and make him long for a vanished world. But the contrast between Tchaikovsky's music and the reality of war destroys the narrator's beautiful dream, and he realizes that romantic illusions about war—and art such as Tchaikovsky's, which fosters them—are dangerous.

"At Night" undoubtedly represents an important stage in Kataev's literary development. Yet it must not be singled out as more important than other stories written at the same time (a fault of most Soviet critics of Kataev's work), for its depressed mood is uncharacteristic of him.[7] To be seen in proper perspective it must be read in conjunction with several other stories and poems written in the same year that show that at this time of war and revolutions Kataev's mood was most often one of youthful optimism. His heroes, including the lyrical hero of his poems, think more frequently of love than they do of war and revolution, and although the theme of war is rarely entirely absent from Kataev's work of 1917, it is most often treated as something that complicates love affairs.

The largely autobiographical story "Baraban" ("The Drum"), dating from Kataev's brief stay in the Odessa Infantry Academy in the spring of 1917, is an amusing tale about a young officer who claims that he can play the big drum in the Academy band although he has never played one in his life. He craves the glory of leading the entire band, and also knows that band members have an extra hour's leave per week, which will give him more time to pursue his current love affair. The indulgent band master is amused by the young man's nerve and allows him to continue his deception.

The hero of "The Drum," Petrov, is a vain dreamer whose ego overwhelms his sense of reality. Yet in the characterization of this largely autobiographical figure there is a disarming warmth and gentle irony which was to become a recurrent feature of the treatment of the many similar figures in Kataev's work. The February Revolution comes as a surprise to the apolitical Petrov, who is cushioned from reality by the Military Academy and by his absorbing love affair. The pattern of the tale, in which the author focuses sharply on the hero's personal problems while sketching in political and social events as an indistinct background, foreshadows similar patterns in such novels as *Lone White Sail* and *Zimnii veter* (*Winter Wind*, 1961). More immediately, Petrov anticipates the heroes of many of Kataev's stories of the Civil War period in that at a time of great social upheaval he thinks only of his own private concerns.

Petrov is the hero of another story of 1917 entitled "A + B v kvadrate" ("A + B Squared"). On the eve of his departure for the front he goes for a walk with his current sweetheart and constantly teases her with a question about mathematics at moments when she expects a declaration of love. The thought that preoccupies both Petrov and the girl—that he might be killed—is suppressed for most of the story behind his defensive screen of flippancy, but in the end he expresses it, thereby resolving the tension in the story and, at the same time, winning conclusively his duel of words and emotions with the girl.

Two stories of 1918, "Chelovek s uzlom" ("The Man with the Bundle") and "Muzyka" ("Music"), show particularly clearly the way in which Kataev's work was being influenced by Bunin. The hero of the former story is a young soldier on guard duty whose thoughts stray to the beauty of the night sky, to poetry, and to the girl he loves. While he is dreaming, a thief breaks into the storehouse and is almost shot by the young soldier. Only the fact that he has forgotten to load his rifle saves him from shooting the thief, and at the end he is badly shaken by the thought of how close he had come to killing. Following the normal pattern for Kataev's stories and poems of this period, war forms the background against which the hero dreams of more beautiful things, but here war breaks suddenly through the web of poetic daydreams spun by the young poet.

Bunin's influence is generally evident in the lyrical descriptive passages and, more particularly, in one striking detail which Kataev borrows from Bunin's story "Legkoe dykhanie" ("Light Breathing"), in which a young girl, confused by her newly awakened sexual feelings, takes off a scarf and covers her face with it. Similarly, in "The Man with the Bundle" the poet recalls how a girl had covered his face with her scarf which smelled sweetly of her hair, and the whole world had appeared lilac through the thin silk. The heightened sensual awareness and the half-concealed sexual excitement in this scene are in direct imitation of Bunin's story, but the younger author does not approach the subtlety of his teacher.

Bunin himself appears as a character at the end of "Music." The story, which has no real plot, attempts to evoke the atmosphere of a very hot afternoon when the narrator is left to look after a little girl whose mother has gone swimming. Most of the story is taken up with the relationship between the narrator and the child. He attempts to amuse and teach her and feels a mixture of tenderness and exasperation toward her. At the end of the story Ivan Alexeevich (clearly Bunin, although the surname is not supplied) comes visiting, and the narrator describes him at length and in detail.

The "music" of the title has a double meaning. First, it refers to the child's confident assertion that she can draw music by scribbling a few strokes on a piece of paper. Second, the child's wish to convey one sense impression (hearing) in terms of another (sight) provides a parallel with Bunin, whose mastery of description is so great that he can find the right words to convey any physical impression. He, too, can paint music by finding the one comparison that will unmistakably suggest to his readers the sound he hears. At the end of the story Kataev portrays Bunin in the act of "drawing music" in this sense: "Ivan Alexeevich stands listening. His expression is one of extreme preoccupation. I know what he is thinking about. He is thinking of a comparison for that long, musical sound of a quivering tram-wire, so like and yet unlike other sounds. A chromatic scale? Perhaps. A cello? Possibly" (I, 134).

Kataev's long description of Bunin in "Music" is an expression of his admiration for the older man's talent, a slightly mocking pastiche, and an attempt to prove himself a worthy pupil by emulating Bunin's powers of description. "It is Ivan Alexeevich. Close-set inkblots of shade from the leaves run swiftly and diagonally down his Tolstoyan blouse of well-ironed linen. On his squeaking, creaking town boots there is a yellow dust from the flowering weeds. There is a stout stick in his hands. A slight upward tilt of the beard. The pince-nez thrust into the top pocket. A proud hooked nose and attentive eyes slightly screwed up" (I, 133).

"Music" has received little attention from critics, yet it must be seen as one of the most significant of Kataev's early works, for it expresses perfectly his aestheticism and also helps to explain the bond between him and Bunin. At a time of national upheaval Bunin and his pupil are concerned solely with finding the precise comparison for the sound of a tram-wire twanging. Although Kataev was to move away from the pure aestheticism of "Music" and, as early as 1921, was to attack this aspect of Bunin's personality in "The Gold Nib," the urge to perfect his powers of description never left him. A straight line of development may be drawn between the twenty-one-year-old author of "Music" and the Kataev of the 1960s, whose minutely accurate descriptions of objects seem to make them almost tangible.

The stories and poems written by Kataev before 1920 represent a considerable achievement for a young author, and in them many of the features of his mature work are already present. But the lucid style he almost invariably employs lacks variety and comes to seem somewhat bland after a while. In the next decade Kataev was to remedy this failing by bolder experimentation and by an infusion of fantasy into his precisely realistic style.

III   *Stories of the Civil War Period*

In 1920 Kataev wrote an impressionistic account of his experiences during the Civil War entitled "Zapiski o grazhdanskoi voine" ("Notes on the Civil War"), which leaves the reader with only a vague idea of the principal historical events of 1919 in Odessa, but with a very clear sense of the atmosphere in the city.[8] It is a city under siege by the Red Army, with the prevailing mood one of hysteria, political uncertainty, and moral decay. Yet, although Kataev writes from a Red point of view he does not conceal his interest in the doomed city, made even more colorful by the intrusion of interventionist forces from four European nations. The style of "Notes on the Civil War" is for the most part straightforward and vigorous, with short sentences and restrained use of imagery, and in this it differs from the purely fictional stories written at the same

time. But in other respects "Notes on the Civil War" may be viewed
as a pendant to such stories as "Opyt Krantsa" ("Krants's Experiment") and "V osazhdennom gorode" ("In the Besieged City"),
which are set in the hysterical atmosphere of an Odessa caught
between White occupants and Red invaders.[9]

The hero of "Krants's Experiment" is a young mathematician who
wishes to prove that he is capable of rejecting or overcoming the
emotional, irrational side of his nature, and of acting entirely in
accordance with rational principles. In order to demonstrate this,
he proposes to win a vast sum at the gambling tables and then to
continue his life as before, quite unaffected by his wealth. The other
major character, a poor actor called Zosin, is present when Krants
wins the first part of his fortune, and learns the details of the mathematician's experiment. Infuriated by the contrast between Krants's
unwanted wealth and his own poverty, he decides to kill Krants and
steal his gold, but finds he is incapable of murder. After two successful evenings, Krants returns for a third attempt at the tables,
and this time loses everything. If his view of his own character had
been correct, he would be unmoved by his loss, but the brief possession of wealth has unleashed subconscious forces in Krants, and
he staggers from the table in a state approaching delirium.

In *The Grass of Oblivion* Kataev recalls reading "Krants's Experiment" to Bunin in the autumn of 1919 (IX, 330). He claimed
that in it he was attempting to apply Bunin's principle of symphonic
prose, but Bunin was not impressed by this point and commented:
"I can no longer see myself in this. You are moving away from me
towards Leonid Andreev." By "symphonic style" Kataev means "the
musical construction of prose, with changes of rhythm, variations,
shifts from one musical key to another—in a word . . . counterpoint"
(IX, 312). This definition of symphonic prose applies more to Kataev's work of the 1960s than to "Krants's Experiment," where the
only sign of a contrapuntal principle is the tension between the two
major characters, the one apparently cold and rational and the other
fevered and irrational. To a certain extent the rhythm of the prose
varies depending upon which character is dominant. For example,
in the opening passage describing Krants the sentences are longer
than usual in Kataev's work of this period, and the adjectives
grouped in threes. "A certain young mathematics student named
Krants—a fair-haired, thick-set chap with a short, firm, Germanic
nose, a stubborn, bony forehead, and widely set eyes—loved pure

mathematics more than anything on earth, and expected nothing from life, neither good nor ill. He loved mathematics because its simple, complex, and precise philosophy was very well suited to his habits and views" (I, 135). In the characterization of Zosin, on the other hand, Kataev attempts to achieve a feverish quality by means of the staccato effect of short phrases. The young author may have attempted to employ a rudimentary contrapuntal technique in imitation of his teacher, but the subtlety of rhythmic variation achieved by Bunin bears little relation to Kataev's simple opposition of two rhythms, inconsistently applied.

For the influences on "Krants's Experiment" one must look elsewhere than to Bunin. Pushkin's "Queen of Spades" and Dostoevsky's *Crime and Punishment* are obvious models. The character of Krants is taken directly from that of Germann, the hero of Pushkin's story, and many details in the gambling scenes come from the same source.[10] The process by which Zosin justifies his idea of murdering Krants recalls some of Raskolnikov's theories. Like Dostoevsky's hero, Zosin views murder as a test of whether he is a man or a nonentity, while simultaneously justifying his plan on the grounds that he needs money whereas Krants does not.

The characters in "Krants's Experiment" may not be original, but they represent an advance for Kataev, for they allow him to introduce elements of delirium and fantasy which combine with the story's realistic features to form a blend that was to become characteristic of Kataev's work of the 1920s. Physical illness, the effects of cocaine, and lust produce in Zosin a state of extreme agitation in which the boundaries between the senses are dissolved, and he sees pictures conjured up by the sounds of an orchestra. Even Krants fails to keep his senses distinct. Like another mathematician—D-503 from Evgeny Zamyatin's *We*—he begins to think in images. When he leaves the tables after losing all, someone tells him that he is holding his cigarette by the wrong end, and he sees the letters of this spoken phrase written in red in his mind's eye.

In *The Grass of Oblivion* Kataev suggests that the major significance of "Krants's Experiment" lies in its evocation of the atmosphere of a doomed bourgeois city, besieged by the Red Army. The first chapter includes an attempt to place the action in time and space by using certain details from "Notes on the Civil War," but once the story of Krants's experiment begins, the social setting becomes irrelevant. Indeed, the final paragraph about the fall of the

city was added by the *Novy mir* editor, Serafimovich, who felt that
the story lacked social significance. The doomed city motif is secondary to the characters and the opportunity which they provide
for verbal experimentation. "Krants's Experiment" could take place
at any time and in any setting; the social contrasts, such as they are,
do no more than add a little poignancy to the plot.

The same can not be said of Kataev's next story, "In the Besieged
City," which shares with "Notes on the Civil War" the atmosphere
of a decadent cosmopolitan city. A drunken sailor stumbles into a
tavern in pursuit of a student whom he takes for a counter-revolutionary spy. The student has been sniffing cocaine—as a result of
which his senses are abnormally acute—and in a state of near ecstasy
he recalls his wonderful life before the Revolution in a world now
irretrievably lost. The sailor then jumps to his feet, denounces the
student as a spy, shoots him dead, and runs out into the street.

The most remarkable feature of this story is the extent to which
Kataev sympathizes with the student (a fact ignored in the mis-
leading discussion by some Soviet critics).[11] It is not clear whether
the student is, indeed, a White Guard agent or whether he is merely
unfortunate enough to be the casual victim of a man crazed by grief
and drink. What is certain, however, is that Kataev sympathizes
with him and shares his tastes to the extent of making him a poet,
whose language resembles Kataev's own. The sailor, in contrast,
remains alien to the author: he is described as "drunk," with "mad
eyes," and there is something incomprehensible and frightening
about him. To imply, as certain critics have, that at this stage of his
career Kataev had already begun consistently to view the Revolution
and Civil War from a Bolshevik point of view is to misinterpret his
work by overlooking the degree of his identification with his central
characters. The young hero of "In the Besieged City" shares with
other heroes of Kataev's Civil War stories a detachment from the
great events of the epoch, a love of poetry and a conviction that it
alone is capable of expressing the beauty of the world, and an acute
awareness of the proximity and irreversibility of death.

"Zheleznoe kol'tso" ("The Iron Ring"), written in 1920 and published in 1923, is one of the best of Kataev's stories of the early
1920s, demonstrating his optimism, his Romantic taste in literature,
and his considerable skill, even at this early stage, as a short story
writer. The theme of the story is common to most of Kataev's work
of this period: human happiness and the beauty of life are constants

which each generation discovers for itself irrespective of particular social conditions. In order to demonstrate the universality of basic human emotions, Kataev uses the figure of the eternal Dr. Faustus to link the time of Pushkin and the present day. Three young poets sit in a bar in Odessa during the Civil War drinking wine and telling tales. One of them tells of how Dr. Faustus and Pushkin once met in Odessa, where the great poet was living in exile. Recognizing in Pushkin a truly happy man, the traveling doctor gave him a simple iron ring with a cheap turquoise stone which had the capacity to make everything around beautiful. Since Pushkin's time many years have passed, but the narrator feels certain that the ring must still be in Odessa because of the way the sun shines and because of the captivating turquoise dust on the plums for sale in the market place. Just as he reaches his conclusion, the narrator and his comrades are joined in the bar by Dr. Faustus, who throws an iron ring onto their table as a sign that he recognizes in them true happiness. They rush into the street after him, but he vanishes, and the ring has also disappeared by the time they return to the inn. They are not downhearted, though, for they are young and they have a bottle of wine and enough lamp oil to while away the rest of the night reading a story by Robert Louis Stevenson.

The iron ring symbolizes the link between Pushkin and the young twentieth-century poets; just as Pushkin manages to overcome his grief at the loss of his mistress, Amalia Riznich, so do the young men shrug off their misfortunes. For Pushkin, as for his young successors, true happiness transcends the varying fortunes of life. The key passage in the story—and a recurrent motif in Kataev's work of the 1920s—consists of Pushkin's words on the nature of happiness:

Who knows what happiness is? Some think that happiness is gold, others believe it to lie in youth and love; there are some idiots who think that happiness is immortality and fame! But, my dear sir, am I happy? If this wind, and the surf, and the light and shade, and the murmur of the waves are happiness, if happiness consists of sails going South, if the nature of human passions is happiness, if everything which fills our poor human life is happiness—then I am happy, and I thank heaven for this imperfect, bitter, beautiful, ordinary human happiness. [I, 166][12]

Kataev's acceptance of life as it is—his view that human happiness is independent of time or social system—forms the philosophical basis of his work of the 1920s. At the end of the decade it would bring him into conflict with the critics of the RAPP group.

Kataev does not identify the three young poets of "The Iron Ring," but it seems likely that they are stylizations of the author himself and two friends, the novelist Yury Olesha (1899–1965) and the poet Eduard Bagritsky (1895–1934).[13] The character of the latter serves as a model for the hero of Kataev's story "Bezdel'nik Eduard" ("Eduard the Loafer"), written in 1920.[14] Among the features that the fictional Eduard Tochkin shares with Bagritsky are his first name, his asthma, his love of Rimbaud and Stevenson, and his interest in ornithology. However, while Kataev undoubtedly had Bagritsky in mind when creating Eduard Tochkin, the character is stylized, a friendly caricature rather than a portrait. As Kataev puts it: "If I'm to tell the tale then I'll tell it without fear of exaggeration or metaphor—in the spirit of that wonderful romantic age" (I, 183).

As an enthusiastic reader of Anatole France, Tochkin greets the October Revolution with fervor, seeing in it a modern version of *Les Dieux ont soif*. When life becomes difficult in the hungry days of the Civil War, he sells most of his mother's possessions and then meets and marries a widow with yet more things for sale. With the money from the sale of her goods he buys books and tobacco, and eventually begins to collect cage birds. Soon the flat is almost emptied of furniture but full of birds, none of which sing. Eduard still fails to see the impending disaster; only his wife's determination and good sense keep them both alive. At the end of the story Eduard has not changed. Unworldly as ever, he still dreams of a house full of singing cage birds.

For all his romantic involvement with the Revolution, Eduard Tochkin remains essentially detached from the great events of the age. At first sight his obsession with birds appears selfish, but his lack of interest in material things for their own sake endears him to the author, whose humor at the character's expense lacks all trace of malice. Although Tochkin resembles Bagritsky rather more than Kataev himself, he elicits from the author an attitude identical to that Kataev adopts toward autobiographical figures, one of warm, affectionate humor and gentle irony.

Another story of 1920, "Ser Genri i chert" ("Sir Henry and the Devil"), affords great scope for fantasy and experimentation, since it consists of the delirious dreams of a typhus victim. At first the sick man retains a weak hold on his consciousness, and is vaguely aware of traveling in a train, of having his head shaved, and of being bathed and put to bed. As his delirium grows more acute, the pain in his ear assumes the form of an interlocutor, a supercilious English student named Sir Henry, who later turns into the captain of a pirate ship. The sick man travels with Sir Henry to an island where there is no soil except gold dust, and where the ordinary earth which he has brought on his boots from the Besieged City is regarded as immensely valuable. Finally, Sir Henry gives way to the Devil, and in the sick man's last moment he hears someone mutter that he has just died.

The principal significance of "Sir Henry and the Devil" lies in its fantastic use of language. Unrestrained by reason or the demands of a conventional plot, Kataev employs imagery reminiscent of the work of the Futurist poets and indulges in nightmarishly sudden changes of scene. The story exhibits that dreamlike fluidity which was to become one of Kataev's distinguishing features in this decade, culminating in one of his best works, the satirical short novel *The Embezzlers*. "Sir Henry and the Devil" opens with a welter of sense impressions which create an effect of disorientation because they are not always connected with their physical causes. "Flaming cigarettes crawled along the railway platform like rockets, scattering sparks and exploding . . . On my head lay a heavy stone, now cold, now hot. Then I was being shaken in a car and the pungent typhus smell of disinfectant mingled with petrol-laden smoke" (I, 173).

Before the intensification of the fever, the hero recalls his three months of service with an armored train and his desire to return to the sweet decadence of the Besieged City. He may be classified as a typical Kataev hero of the period, to whom the war and the revolutionary cause mean less than his former way of life. Other links with contemporary stories include the theme of the obsessive desire for wealth (here "made strange" by the reversal of the values of soil and gold);[15] the resonances from Robert Louis Stevenson; and the awareness of the closeness and irreversibility of death. Due, no doubt, to the chance nature of life and death in wartime and to Kataev's own narrow escapes from death by typhus and at the hands of a band of terrorists, the theme of the uniqueness of each individual's life and the finality of death is particularly prevalent in his work of the first half of the 1920s.

Kataev has recently linked his work of the 1960s with "Sir Henry and the Devil," suggesting that the story represented a first attempt

at a style of writing that he longed to master, but that he was forced
to drop because of the increasing hostility in the late 1920s and
early 1930s to fantasy and extravagant style. Only in recent years
has he found it possible to return to this type of writing.[16]

IV Two Transitional Stories

Of the stories written in the first half of the 1920s two stand out
by virtue of their serious tone and their personal subject matter.
"Otets" ("The Father") and "Zimoi" ("In Winter") mark a transition
in Kataev's work to full independence and maturity.

Kataev once described "The Father" as his favorite story, and he
worked on it for three years, from 1922 to 1925, before submitting
it to the journal *Krasnaya nov (Red Virgin Soil)* for publication.[17]
The story opens with the hero, Petr Sinaysky, sitting in prison,
waiting for his case to be reviewed by the Bolshevik criminal investigator. His widowed father, racked by anxiety for his son, stands
for hours outside the prison hoping to catch a glimpse of him at one
of the windows. After several months Petr's case is investigated and
he is released. In the first flush of gratitude and relief he vows never
again to worry his father; but his good intentions soon fade and
before long he finds life with the old man tedious and leaves home.
His father has to live with a niece while Petr lives alone in a comfortable room. When spring comes, Petr is sent on official business
to the surrounding villages. His father, who fears that the young
man will be killed by one of the marauding bands which still ter-
rorize the countryside, pleads in vain with him not to go. During
the son's absence the old man dies and, on his return to the city,
Petr sells all of his father's possessions and travels North to begin
a new life.

In Kataev's presentation of the relationship between father and
son, the autobiographical figure, Petr, is not spared. His selfishness
emerges most clearly in the scene in which the father visits his new
apartment in the hope of being asked to stay and is sent on his way
with nothing more than a cup of coffee. Yet, for all Kataev's insistence on the selfishness of Petr's behavior, he does not condemn
his character, for he sees the impatience and thoughtlessness of
youth as a natural part of life and, therefore, as something to be
accepted. As one hostile critic put it: "Nature is cruel, but it is

beautiful in its cruelty. Old age is pitiful and disgusting, and nature rejects it. The son is correct because he is full of the joy of life."[18]

Sinaysky's awareness of the goodness of life in all its complexity is heightened by the possibility of his imminent execution. "The prison was visible from the cemetery. The cemetery was visible from the prison. That was the way the ends tied up in life, in this surprising, bitter and beautiful, ordinary human life!" (1,222) On the journey from the prison to the investigator's office where his fate will be determined, Petr marvels at the beauty of the huge expanse of damp, fertile earth; at the branches touched by the yellow of autumn; at the air, bluish and misty like a soap bubble. Similarly, the death of his father, much as it saddens him, also liberates him. He feels like a man just discharged from the hospital, to whom the world seems both empty and fresh. Through the act of selling his father's books Sinaysky simultaneously experiences grief and an invigorating freedom, and Kataev seems to be saying that this is a natural reaction. The final chapter, consisting of one fairly short sentence, recapitulates and crystallizes the main point of the story: "And the sky, like the unforgettable face of his father, wept over the son a flood of warm, joyful stars" (I, 255). Nature condones and even approves Sinaysky's behavior toward his father.

Critics have sometimes claimed that Kataev's characterization lacks psychological veracity.[19] In the main, it is true that the creation of psychologically convincing adult characters is not one of Kataev's strong points, but in "The Father" he does succeed in suggesting the inner state of both major figures, largely by describing external, physical details. As has been pointed out by one critic, no less a writer than Turgenev frequently approaches characterization in a similar way.[20] Sinaysky's father appears to his son for most of the story as a pathetic, abject old man with a whining, pitiful voice; yet when the point of view shifts from the son, the old man appears in a different light, as an earnest and dignified person grown old and forgetful, but still worthy of respect. The multiplicity of viewpoint (Petr's present view, his recollections of his father as a younger man, and the view of the niece, Darya) establishes a complex and convincing picture of the father, although he is viewed almost entirely from the outside.

Besides the characterization, "The Father" is notable for its ornate imagery and Kataev's careful attention to the auditory effect of the work. Many of the images function on the principle of comparing

something unknown and frightening to something familiar and re-
assuring, especially in the section devoted to Petr's recollections
of childhood. Thus his mother's coffin resembles a large cake, and
slides into the funeral carriage like a photographic plate sliding into
a camera. Some of the images seem calculated to shock in a way
that was common in Soviet literature of the 1920s. Mayakovsky,
Babel, Sholokhov, and many lesser writers all used grotesque imagery from time to time. For example, such images as those in the
following passage from "The Father" were part of the common
currency of the period: "And the evening, lit by a candle-stub in
the neck of a black bottle, guttered in the azure and gold of stearin
and melted on to the limp pieces of peel, and the yellow diarrhoea
of melon flesh spread out on the table" (I, 218).

In his use of imagery in this story Kataev occasionally seems to
be striving for effect, but on the whole "The Father" is an impressive
creation, combining seriousness of purpose, good characterization,
and a richly textured style.

The hero of the autobiographical story "In Winter" is a stylized
version of Kataev himself, rather as Eduard Tochkin is a stylization
of Bagritsky.[21] The story tells of an intense five-day love affair between a young poet and the sister of a fellow writer who has come
to Moscow from her native Kiev for a short winter holiday.[22] While
it lasts, the passion dominates the young man's life, preventing him
from eating, sleeping, or working. After the girl has returned to
Kiev, the poet informs her brother that he intends to marry her,
and, stung by the brother's incredulous scorn at his poverty, he
works frantically, sells a number of stories and poems, and makes
a considerable sum of money. When he visits the girl in Kiev, he
discovers that she has returned to her former way of life and now
has no intention of marrying him. The affair, however, although
short-lived, brings about an important change in the hero. For a
while he recalls with nostalgia the heady days of the Revolution and
Civil War, and the present seems gloomy; but then he reaches a
state of hope in which he can face the future with the knowledge
of his own ability and independence.

It is worth noting that the style of "In Winter," intended to convey
the feverish intensity of the hero's passion, resembles that of the
Five Year Plan novel *Time, Forward!*, in which Kataev also seeks
to describe feverish activity. In both works he employs staccato
rhythms and the device of listing objects in order to create an

impression of urgency. Kataev has acknowledged Mayakovsky's influence on *Time, Forward!*, and "In Winter" also resembles the work of the Futurist poet, especially his long poem about the pain of unrequited love, *Pro eto* (*About That*, 1923). Mayakovsky's poem appeared in print one month before "In Winter," and although it may not have directly influenced Kataev's story, the parallels between the two are striking.[23] In both, the effect of love is deranging; both deal with the reestablishment of bourgeois values in the NEP period; both are permeated with a nostalgia for the idealism of the Revolution and Civil War period; finally, both end with an upturn of hope, although of a different nature. Mayakovsky's poem concludes with a utopian view of man's future, whereas "In Winter" ends with the hero's confident and realistic appraisal of his own worth. One sentence in the story comes almost straight from another Mayakovsky poem, *Oblako v shtanakh* (*A Cloud in Trousers*, 1915): "And the crossed-off, lived-through days jump from the squares of the calendar, like people out of the windows of a burning house" (I, 292–93).

An earlier title of the story—"The Triumphant Brass"—refers to one of its principal motifs, the brass section of an orchestra. In Chapter 2 the penniless, lovesick hero is drawn to the one place in Moscow which he associates with the girl—the park where they always meet. Depressed by his lack of food and tobacco and by the prospect of having to wait four hours before he can see the girl, when he meets an acquaintance he suggests to him that the brass section of an orchestra which they can hear is weeping over lost youth and happiness. His acquaintance, who has money in his pocket and a comfortable home, rejects the young writer's view, and counters that the brass sounds triumphant. This contrast is used several times in the story, almost like a graph, to chart the hero's mood. At the end he reaches the conclusion that the brass section is triumphant and tearful by turns. In other words, he realizes that the past will continue to exert a power over him, that he will continue to regret the passing of youth, but that, equally, he will look forward exultantly to the future. The past, the hero's youth, and the weeping of the brass are all associated in the story's imagery with the Southwest; whereas, the future, the hero's career as a writer, and the exultant notes of the brass section are associated with Moscow in the Northeast. Time after time Kataev returns to the geographical distance between Moscow and the Ukraine, which correlates with a distinction in the hero's life between past and future.

Thus, the theme of "In Winter," like that of "The Father," revolves about the process of maturing. For both heroes a pressing problem is to strike a balance between past and future, between South and North. While the South will always be linked with youth and remain an important part of life, the North is full of potential for the future.

V *Two Early Positive Heroes?*

The typical hero of Kataev's Civil War stories supported the Revolution—if he did at all—because of its romantic associations, but he stopped short of formal allegiance to the Bolshevik party, and was interested more in love and poetry than in politics. With the heroes of "Ogon' " ("Fire") and "Rodion Zhukov," however, the pattern appears to be broken, in that both are committed to the workers' cause and neither bears any superficial resemblance to the predominating intellectual dreamer type. Yet the difference is more apparent than real, for in at least one important respect—their temporary derangement—these heroes conform to the typical pattern of Kataev's work in this decade.

The terse and dramatic opening sentence of "Fire" (written in 1922 but published only in 1927) introduces the plot as succinctly as possible and serves to intrigue the reader: "Katya, the wife of the Communist Erokhin, was burned to death" (I, 260). Until the death of his wife in a tragic accident Erokhin pursues his work of writing anti-religious propaganda with great energy; but the shock of her death robs him, at least temporarily, of the conviction that religion is nothing but superstitious nonsense. While wandering around the town in a state bordering on madness, he finds himself drawn to the church, which he enters just in time to hear the priest denounce him and thank God for killing his wife. So powerful an emotion does this awaken in him that he feels compelled to go to the priest's house to discuss Katya's death. In desperation he asserts that this was not a divine punishment, but simply an accident of a type that will be eliminated in the future, when oil has been replaced as the basic fuel. On leaving the priest's home, he returns to his hut to write another anti-religious pamphlet, but soon falls asleep and dreams of floating higher and higher through the atmosphere to colder and colder regions in search of God. But God and the angels do not exist; there is only "Cold. Ice. Silence. Fire. Death . . ." (I, 274).

As with most of Kataev's heroes, Erokhin's life is so severely disrupted that his normal way of looking at the world becomes distorted.[24] His wife's death causes him to question the rational, materialistic nature of his philosophy, although he does not consciously admit his doubts. Thus, as with the mathematician in "Krants's Experiment," a struggle takes place within Erokhin between the dominant trait of rationality and subsconscious irrational forces released by a traumatic experience. Erokhin's reason tells him that there is no God, and that death is simply the change of matter from one state to another; but his emotions of love, grief, and guilt cannot be explained by reason, and they engender the wish that Katya could still be alive with God. The story's two fundamental motifs of ice and fire correspond to the rational and irrational sides of Erokhin's character. The dream at the end of the story is a particularly skillful blend of reason and irrationality, of realism and fantasy. In the dream Erokhin continues to write the anti-religious pamphlet on which he had been engaged before falling asleep: "We rise higher still. The sun becomes brighter. The air is colder. It is already difficult to breathe. But we go higher, higher! The sun grows huge above our heads. It already covers half the sky. And the sky itself has faded and grown pale. There is no trace of its fine blue color. It is cold. It burns with its coldness . . ." (I, 274). In the end, ice appears to conquer fire, but although Erokhin may return to his normal mental state (there are hints that he will quickly regain his rationality), the author has revealed the power of the subconscious, and it is clear that the "fire" of the title does not simply refer to the accident that killed Katya.

Until "Rodion Zhukov" (written in 1925 and published the following year), the heroes of all Kataev's mature stories belonged to the same generation as the author himself.[25] With this story he turns for the first time to an earlier generation and a subject that was already history (although, significantly, his memories of childhood provide many details).

Rodion Zhukov is a member of the crew of the battleship *Potemkin* who finds life unbearable in Rumania (where the mutinous crew surrendered) and returns to his homeland, only to be arrested as soon as he steps ashore in Odessa. The major part of the story

concerns Zhukov's journey on foot and by boat from Constanza to
Odessa. Although he regrets the surrender of the *Potemkin* and
although he intends to work as an underground revolutionary on
his return to Russia, Zhukov is by no means the self-confident
Communist hero of the same name who appears in the tetralogy
Volny Chernogo moria (*Black Sea Waves*, 1936–61). His desire to
return to Russia is prompted less by a wish to continue the revolutionary struggle than by an instinctive longing for home. Significantly, the predominant motif in the story is that of blindness.
Even before the onset of his fever, Rodion's journey takes on the
features of a blind man's walk: "And Rodion knew even less than
he had in Rumania of what was happening in Russia. He found his
way by guesswork, anxious and alone, like a blind man, tirelessly
walking on so as to get to the mouth of the Dnestr as soon as
possible" (I, 314). On reaching the Danube, he comes across a group
of boys wading in a shallow pool and catching freshwater fish which
have been swept out to sea in a storm, blinded by the salt water,
then trapped behind a sandbank. Zhukov plunges into the water
to catch some fish and, as a result, contracts a fever. The fish,
blinded and swept along by an irresistible force, symbolize the fate
of Zhukov who, acting purely by instinct, is swept into a trap from
which he cannot escape.

For the whole of the second half of "Rodion Zhukov" the hero
suffers from delirium, and the normal passage of time and movement
in space, carefully established earlier in the tale, give way to a
mental state in which events on board the *Potemkin* are interspersed
with what is actually happening to Zhukov on his journey. The
debilitating fever adds greatly to the passivity which is the hero's
major characteristic. Kataev sympathizes with Zhukov, but he is
interested more in portraying a man in a state of derangement than
in glorifying the bravery of a positive hero. Eleven years later, when
Kataev incorporated much of "Rodion Zhukov" into his novel *Lone
White Sail*, he transformed the sick, passive man of the story into
a brave, resourceful positive hero. Of course, to some extent this
difference may be explained by the fact that *Lone White Sail* is an
adventure novel for children, but probably more important are the
differences in the general literary climate and in Kataev's own attitude (two closely related factors) between 1925 and 1936. In the
earlier period it was possible to portray a working-class hero as the
passive victim of circumstance, whereas in the mid-1930s it was not.

This point is worth emphasizing because the importance of "Rodion Zhukov" in Kataev's development as a committed Soviet author has been exaggerated by some critics.[26] If the picture of the hero remains free from the features added in *Lone White Sail*, then "Rodion Zhukov" cannot be seen as heralding a change of the author's direction. Zhukov and Erokhin may belong to a different class from most of Kataev's heroes and may not share their love of poetry, but his treatment of them reveals no other significant change in his interests and intentions.

VI *"The Child"*

Kataev's last important story of the 1920s—"Rebenok" ("The Child," 1929)—could have been merely sentimental, but its humor and charming characterization make it one of the author's best short stories. An unsophisticated young girl named Polechka works as domestic help for a music teacher and conductor called Lyudvig Yakovlevich Knigge. After quarrelling with her landlady, she moves, unbidden, into his room, sleeping behind the curtain that divides it into two sections. Despite the differences in their ages and interests, Polechka and Lyudvig Yakovlevich fall in love, but neither dares admit it to the other. One night, however, when both are in bed, Polechka cannot help groaning with passion. Her employer mistakes her groans for symptoms of a real illness and calls to a neighbor to bring in some medicine. After this incident Polechka becomes pregnant by the local barber, who plans to use the fact that she lives in the same room as Lyudvig Yakovlevich to obtain a paternity order against the conductor. To the barber's astonishment and Polechka's incredulous delight, Lyudvig Yakovlevich admits responsibility for the child in court and expresses his willingness to marry Polechka.

The characters of Polechka and Lyudvig Yakovlevich are lightly sketched in with the use of two devices which had, by this time, become standard features of Kataev's method: the revelation of personality by means of external detail; and a warmly humorous attitude toward the characters. Both features may be seen in the description of the daily routine of changing for the evening performance, which is a highly charged situation for both characters. Every day Lyudvig Yakovlevich's boots fall to the floor because, in his anxiety not to touch Polechka's hand lest she should think he is making advances, he drops them just before she manages to catch hold of them.

"The Child" was published at a time when works of literature on so-called "personal" themes were under severe attack by critics of the RAPP group. Doubtless for this reason, the editor of the journal which first published "The Child" attached a curiously defensive foreword to the story: "The subject of Valentin Kataev's story appears at first sight to be an insignificant domestic incident. Yet this tragicomic event is narrated with such subtle irony and observation that not only are the reader's full attention and interest held by the characters, but he is also forced to think seriously about several features of our everyday lives."[27] That such a note should be necessary reveals that Soviet literature, like Soviet society, was changing very rapidly at the end of the 1920s. Fellow-travelers like Kataev found their works coming increasingly under attack from hostile critics, unwilling to accept any longer the type of theme and approach favored by the fellow-traveler. But before discussing in more detail how the changes in the literary climate at the end of the 1920s affected Kataev, we must discuss the other strand of his work in that decade—his satire.

CHAPTER 3

The Fellow-Traveler: Satire

SOVIET satire flourished during the NEP period. The relative
freedom from official intervention in literature combined with
the evident contradictions between the aspirations of the young
Soviet state and its current economic system to produce a rich
breeding ground for satire. Vladimir Mayakovsky, Mikhail Zoshchenko, Mikhail Bulgakov, Mikhail Koltsov, Ilya Ilf, Evgeny Petrov,
and Ilya Ehrenburg all produced satirical works of high quality,
ranging in length from poems or sketches of a few lines to novels
and plays. The aim of some Soviet satirists was obviously to point
to imperfections in the hope of helping to rectify them. Mayakovsky
and Koltsov, for instance, were passionately committed politically,
and their conviction adds a sharp edge to their satire. In Zoshchenko's tragicomic miniature stories, too, a note of passionate concern can often be heard, although it is of a moral rather than a
political nature. On the other hand, some of the cleverest satirists
of the 1920s remained detached from the circumstances that they
described, recording with sardonic amusement, but with no pain,
the absurdities of life in the NEP period. It is to this latter category
that Kataev belongs. With few exceptions his work lacks the "firm
ideological or moral base" which one critic sees as essential to the
best Soviet satire.[1] But in spite of his lack of a sense of outrage,
Kataev must be counted among the foremost satirists of the decade,
for his work is always accomplished and almost always amusing. In
recent years leading Soviet experts on satire have accorded Kataev
a significant place among satirical writers of his generation,[2] and in
the West he has sometimes been viewed primarily as a satirist.[3]

I "The Gold Nib"

Kataev's first major satirical story was written in 1920, while he
was working as a journalist in Kharkov. The principal character and

49

butt of the satire in "The Gold Nib" is academician Shevelev—a thin disguise for Bunin. Thus, the story, which was written just two years after "Music," represents the first clear sign in Kataev's work of an ambiguous response to the artistry of his mentor. More than forty years later, in *The Grass of Oblivion*, Kataev examined in detail his ambivalent attitude toward Bunin, but that attitude can already be inferred from the two portraits in "Music" and "The Gold Nib." In the former story Kataev admires and seeks to emulate the master (although there is just a hint of sarcasm); in the latter he never questions the beauty of Shevelev's/Bunin's prose, but he emphasizes the huge gulf between the academician and those ordinary people whose lives are being improved by the Revolution which Shevelev so resolutely opposes.

Academician Shevelev, a famous writer, lives in a city under siege. Just as the city is about to fall to the Reds, he locks himself in his study to write a story about a dying prince. He leaves his desk just twice a day—once for his customary walk and once for dinner. When the position of the city has already become hopeless, he agrees to help the White commander by writing an article for the local newspaper calling on the people to oppose the Reds. But the city falls to the besieging army, and Shevelev's life is spared only because of his importance to Russian literature.[4]

The academician is an aristocratic figure with long, parchment-colored fingers and a bony, aquiline skull. He is believed to have an intimate understanding of the common people, but, in fact, he devotes so much time to polishing the style of his stories that he fails to perceive their real attitude to him and the Reds. So engrossed is he in the art of writing that he becomes totally identified with the gold nib of his fountain pen: nothing else matters to him. Consequently there is an unbridgeable gap between the beautiful, economically written, highly polished lines about the dying prince on the one hand, and the fate of the town and its inhabitants on the other.

Given his devotion to art for its own sake, Shevelev might be expected to remain neutral in the political and military struggle raging in the city, but this is not the case. Blinded to political reality by his single-minded pursuit of aesthetic aims, he changes from a cold, detached artist into a fanatical and dangerous enemy of the common people. His stiff, regular behavior gives way to a surprising passion: "He clenched his fists and, with raised head and flashing eyes, and ready to bite off the head of anyone who might dare to cross the threshold of his room, he waited for the end" (I, 164).

For all the sarcastic, satirical coloration with which Kataev portrays Shevelev, there is a grandeur in the academician's single-mindedness and the mad obstinacy of his refusal to accept a passage to Paris which raises him far above the unidimensional figures in Kataev's other satirical works of the early 1920s. Clearly, Kataev's closeness to Bunin enables him to go beyond merely superficial characterization, and to write his only satirical story of the first half of the 1920s which is based on character rather than on situation.

Significantly, the weakness of "The Gold Nib" lies in the attempt to portray the band of Red sailors and soldiers who come to arrest Shevelev: "The academician walked to the window. He could clearly see these jolly, raggedly-dressed soldiers with red arm-bands, and the sailors' leather jackets" (I, 164). Kataev's own uncertainty tells in the confusion of point of view and in his complete lack of individualization of the Reds. The point of view in the passage appears to be that of Shevelev ("he could clearly see"), yet the soldiers are described as "jolly"—an inappropriate adjective for the threatened writer to use. With the central character, based on a man whom he knew well, Kataev experiences no difficulties; but with the Reds, whom he attempts to portray in a positive light without understanding them, he loses his way.

"The Gold Nib" may be considered a betrayal of Bunin.[5] Yet, as a satirical story based on character its high quality is undeniable. If it reveals in Kataev an ambiguous attitude toward the Revolution, a readiness to adapt to changing circumstances, and a preparedness to portray a friend in a negative light, it also shows him to be a good satirical writer.

II *Short Satirical Sketches*

In the 1920s Kataev published in various newspapers and journals several hundred satirical short stories, sketches (*fel'etony*), and verses. Many of these were written in response to a news item or a reader's letter of complaint. For example, one of the best of the prose sketches—"Beremennyi muzhchina" ("The Pregnant Man," 1926)—bears as an epigraph a news report about the difficult working conditions of doctors in the Railway Medical Service, who sometimes have to deal with up to one hundred and fifty patients each

day. The report claims that one overworked doctor in the Vologda
region diagnosed pregnancy in a male patient. Taking this incident
as his subject, Kataev writes a dialogue between a male patient and
a harassed doctor who persists in diagnosing pregnancy despite the
patient's objections. The sketch ends with a plea to ease the load
of doctors "before every male staff member on the railways begins
giving birth" (II, 331).

"The Pregnant Man" illustrates several recurrent features of Kataev's satirical sketches of the 1920s.[6] First, there is little or no
description of scene or character; only the situation is developed,
and that purely by means of dialogue. Second, that situation lends
itself to a comic treatment. And third, the satire is mild because of
the author's attitude of tolerant amusement.

In "Borodatyi maliutka" ("The Bearded Infant," 1924), which satirizes sensational journalism, a reporter photographs a bearded baby
in order to attract readers to his newspaper, and then shaves the
child to prevent other newspapers from printing the same story.
The hero of "Kozel v ogorode" ("A Wolf among the Sheep," 1923)
is the speaker at an abstinence rally who is himself drunk, and who
only interests his audience when he tells them how to distil vodka.
In "Vyderzhal" ("He Passed," 1924) the practice of examining em-
ployees on political matters is held up to ridicule. A clerk in a Soviet
commercial organization desperately tries to learn a mass of political
information parrot-fashion, so that he can survive a purge of "politically illiterate workers," but in the event he becomes so confused
that his answers do not correspond to the questions asked, with
amusing results. "Chudo kooperatsii" ("A Miracle of Cooperation,"
1924) mocks the habit of praising cooperative labor by applying the
well-known slogan which is the title of the sketch to an argument
between four "suspects" in a paternity suit. "Samoubiitsa ponevole"
("The Unwilling Suicide," 1926) is an old tale given a new twist by
being set in Soviet Russia at a time when the quality of consumer
products was lamentable. Disillusioned with life, a Soviet citizen
decides to commit suicide, but his intention is thwarted by the
inadequacy of the implements he uses. A rope snaps, a nail breaks,
a knife proves insufficiently stout to penetrate the skin, a box of
matches contains so few that he is unable to poison himself. When
he smashes his head against a wall, the bricks collapse. Finally,
when the mood of despair passes and he no longer wishes to end
his life, he eats some contaminated sausage and dies of food poi-
soning.

These works are representative of a large number of Kataev's short satirical sketches and stories. On the surface, they resemble those of Zoshchenko, but the work of the two men springs from very different sources. Zoshchenko's ludicrous stories are the work of a frustrated idealist with a tragic view of his fellow men. Kataev, on the other hand, sees only the ridiculous side of the gulf between aspirations and reality, never its tragedy.

Kataev's sketches have a harder edge when they deal with the abuse of Party membership or working-class status, or with the attitude of foreigners to the USSR. The former theme—known in Russian as *komchvanstvo* (Communist swagger)—occurs in the work of Mayakovsky (notably in his play *The Bedbug*, in which a boorish lout makes use of his prestigious trade-union ticket to marry into a rich bourgeois family). Similarly, in Kataev's "Zagadochnyi Sasha" ("The Mysterious Sasha," 1924) a young working-class man imagines that his proletarian origins will ensure him a place in college and confidently takes the entrance examination without any preparation. The hero of "Tovarishch Probkin" ("Comrade Probkin," 1924) designates his own home a commune and furnishes it with government money. His family—the members of the "model October Revolution Commune"—have access to such "communal facilities" as "the music section" (a piano), the "Marxist library" (a collection of books published by the well-known prerevolutionary publishing firm of Marx and Co.), the "zoological section" (a parrot and a goldfish)—and all bought with state funds allotted to the "commune"!

If Kataev's innate good humor is strained by the abuse of Party membership or working-class status, it is occasionally totally dispelled by the aggressive attitude of foreigners toward his country. His patriotism provides the passionate indignation that sharpens his satire. In "Upriamyi amerikanets" ("A Stubborn American," 1923) an American tourist denigrates the achievements of the Soviet Union and insists that ninety-nine per cent of Russians have no shirts to wear under their jackets. When challenged to prove his allegations, he asks passersby to remove their jackets: all have shirts except one, who turns out to be a foreigner.

Some of Kataev's sketches about foreign politicians resemble the work of prominent Soviet cartoonists. For example, he portrays the British politicians Winston Churchill, Neville Chamberlain, Ramsay MacDonald, and Stanley Baldwin as the lackeys of powerful capitalists and the aristocratic establishment. One such verbal cartoon, "Parad pobeditelei" ("The Victors' Parade," 1926), depicts Arthur

Henderson, Baldwin, and MacDonald as wrestlers and King George
V as the referee who establishes the rules and allows foul holds as
he wishes.[7]

III   Two Parody Adventure Novels

In the early 1920s adventure novels modelled on the work of such
Western authors as Jules Verne, Conan Doyle, and H. G. Wells
enjoyed great popularity with Soviet readers. Under the pseudonym
of Jim Dollar, Marietta Shaginyan wrote the enormously successful
Mess-Mend: A Yankee in Petrograd, an example of what became
known as "Red Pinkerton literature," i.e., detective fiction with a
Communist hero instead of the typical "private eye" like Nat Pinkerton. Shaginyan soon had her imitators, and dozens of "Red Pinkerton" novels, in which detection and revolution went side by side,
were published by private and state publishing houses.[8] A slightly
different type of popular novel combined the themes of science
fiction writers like H. G. Wells with the theme of the downfall of
capitalism and the birth of a new revolutionary society.[9] The best
of these adventure novels contained elements of satire and parody,
as in Ilya Ehrenburg's *The Unusual Adventures of Julio Jurenito*
(1922) and *The D.E. Trust: The Downfall of Europe* (1923).

Kataev, too, joined the rush to write adventure novels,[10] but the
two that he wrote in 1924 and 1925 are not straightforward examples
of the genre. Both *Ostrov Erendorf (Erendorf Island)* and *Povelitel'
zheleza (The Master of Iron)* illustrate Kataev's love of parody and
satire, and neither should (or could) be taken seriously, as the al-
leged date of composition of the former work—April 1, 1924—
shows. In the opening chapter of *Erendorf Island* Kataev lists the
conventions that the reader has now come to expect of this kind of
novel and assures him that he will not be disappointed:

Having read the opening lines about an ancient professor making some
very complex calculations and agitatedly wiping his graying temples with
his large professorial handkerchief, the reader is, of course, fully entitled
to adopt a sceptical attitude to my novel, and to give up reading it at the
first page. It would be difficult to object to this. Of course, the reader
already knows in advance that the professor makes a brilliant discovery
which ought to benefit mankind. Naturally some villains steal the formulas
and diagrams which the naive scientist had produced in a single copy. [II,
490]

The tongue-in-cheek tone of the opening passage is maintained throughout the novel, the plot of which revolves about the discovery by an eminent geologist that tidal waves will soon destroy the entire world with the exception of a tiny island in the Atlantic Ocean. In his concern to save mankind, he takes his discovery to Matapal, the world's most powerful capitalist, who is at that moment locked in a desperate struggle with trade unionists under their leader Paich. Realizing that capitalism is doomed, Matapal sees in the professor's discovery an opportunity to create a perfect capitalist society on the island. However, he and his retinue are drowned when only the island is destroyed and the rest of the world remains untouched by the sea. The mistake arose because the firm that produced the professor's new adding machine had inadvertently transposed the plus and minus signs.

The parody in *Erendorf Island* is of H. G. Wells and, more particularly, of Ilya Ehrenburg, whose name is hinted at in the title of Kataev's work. In Ehrenburg's *The D.E. Trust* a group of powerful American capitalists set up an organization for the destruction of Europe. One of them—a Mr. Jebbs—resembles Matapal in that both organize their lives on a very strict timetable,[11] setting aside one hour per day for the purpose of interviewing inventors whose ideas might prove useful to their capitalist empires. There can be no doubt that Kataev aims to parody Ehrenburg in *Erendorf Island*, and as a skit on a popular genre of the time the novel proves quite successful. Similarly, so long as the satire in the work remains on the level of the caricature of capitalism (in the cartoon style of some of the short sketches), it is accomplished and amusing. But as soon as Kataev tries to depict the victims of an evil capitalism in a realistic fashion, the work's fragile structure—which rests on the author's knowing urbanity—crashes to the ground. There is no room in *Erendorf Island* for a straightforward description of oppressed workers.

The Master of Iron, published in the small provincial town of Veliky Ustyug and never republished in full, is one of the least known of Kataev's works. The plot is more complex than that of *Erendorf Island*, although the basic elements are the same: a clash between capitalists and workers (in Calcutta this time) and a scientific discovery which will affect the future of mankind. The "master of iron" of the title is a Moscow scientist who has acquired a machine which will magnetize all metal objects and so render in-

effective all machinery, including armaments. Sickened by his experiences of war, he retreats to Tibet and from there issues a warning
to all governments to stop fighting. Unfortunately, his machine
seems likely to thwart a revolution in India until he is discovered
and defeated. The two major subplots involve Stanley, the inept
nephew of Sherlock Holmes, who is engaged to track down the
Indian revolutionary leader Ramashandra, and Korolev, a Moscow
journalist who attempts to find the mysterious "master of iron" in
order to interview him.

Apart from his obvious debt to Jules Verne's *Master of the World*
and to Conan Doyle, Kataev once again parodies Ehrenburg and
the writers of sensational novels about death rays which were in
vogue in 1924–25. For example, Ehrenburg's *The D.E. Trust*
proved so popular that it was adapted for the stage (and produced
by no less a figure than Meyerhold), and a cigarette company even
produced a brand of cigarettes called D.E.[12] Kataev mocks this kind
of popularity in a passage from *The Master of Iron*: "Naturally
enough, Master of Iron brand cigarettes and suspenders came immediately onto the market. No fewer than two thousand dramatists
swiftly re-wrote their comedies to include the Master of Iron among
the dramatis personae . . . Everyone made money out of the Master
of Iron—everyone was happy."[13]

Like *Erendorf Island, The Master of Iron* succeeds as a parody
of other works and as a light satire on capitalism and imperialism.
Once again, however, the unity of tone is destroyed with the introduction of a positive hero, Ramashandra, who eulogizes the Russian Revolution: "And until nightfall Ramashandra told his sweetheart
wonderful legends about a white man who had given his life for
oppressed people. The name of that man was Lenin."[14]

Kataev's two parody novels played an important part in the development of the genre: indeed, one leading specialist in this field
dates the beginning of the Soviet parody novel from these works.[15]
Moreover, they demonstrate Kataev's liking for combining satire,
literary parody, and an adventure novel plot in one work—a combination he was to return to in his major creation of the 1920s, *The
Embezzlers*.

IV "*Things*"

The longer satirical stories written by Kataev in the second half
of the 1920s all have money or goods as an important element in

them. During this period his satirical censure of the love of wealth intensified, but it never entirely subdued his characteristic sympathy for men and women in the grip of an obsessive desire to be rich.

The least attractive of such characters is the fairground booth owner in "Nozhi" ("Toss-the-Hoop," 1926).[16] In this story a young man called Pasha visits a fairground on a fine summer evening and sees a girl at a toss-the-hoop stall. He falls instantly in love, courts her and proposes marriage, but her father refuses his permission because Pasha has no capital to expand the fairground business. Seeing no other way to secure his happiness, Pasha practices tossing the hoop all winter with the intention of bankrupting the owner when the fairground opens again in spring. This he does, and the girl's father, forced to choose between her and his wealth, gives up his daughter to her beloved Pasha.

"Nozhi" combines the two major strains of Kataev's work of the 1920s in that it is both lyrical and satirical. For the young lovers Moscow is the most romantic of cities, a place in which the trees blossom and the moon shines brightly in a deep purple sky; but for the booth owner Moscow means nothing more than money. He has "strong passions" (to use Kataev's phrase) no less than the younger man, but his have been displaced from fellow humans to money and goods.

A similar displacement of passion is the subject of one of the best of Kataev's stories, "Veshchi" ("Things"), which, although written in 1929 after the NEP period had formally ended, belongs in spirit to that era. The central characters are a young couple called Zhorzhik and Shurka who are married on a fine May day. Straight after the wedding they rush to the market to buy "things," such as blankets, goloshes, an alarm clock, chairs, a rug with a tiger on it, and much else besides. During the next few months Shurka often wakes in the night and thinks of things she could have bought. Whenever they receive their pay they rush to the market to supplement their stock of goods. Meanwhile, Zhorzhik's health begins to deteriorate, but in the face of neighbors' warnings that he needs hospital treatment Shurka insists she can look after him. When he dies, she is genuinely grief-stricken, but after a while she meets another young man, marries him, and goes straight to the market to buy things.

The major satirical device in this story is the displacement of the normal passion of a young wife for her husband by Shurka's passion for things. After the wedding, Zhorzhik hints to his wife that they should find a place to be alone, but she has other things on her mind: " 'Where shall we go now?' asked the meek, lanky, skinny Zhorzhik, casting a sidelong glance at Shurka. Big, beautiful, and as warm as a stove, she squeezed up against him, tickling his ear with the cherry twig which she had stuck in her thinning hair. With nostrils passionately flared, she whispered, 'To Sukharevka Market. To buy things. Where else would we go?' " (I, 362). Later on, when they are lying in bed, the strength of her emotions prevents her from sleeping: "Shurka woke in the night and, tormented by secret desires, she roused her husband. 'Listen, Zhorzhik . . . Zhorzhik, darling . . . , she whispered, and her breath was hot on his collarbone. 'Wake up! You know it's a pity we didn't buy that yellow blanket' " (I, 364).

Kataev adds depth to his characterization by making Shurka a not unsympathetic figure. She is not indifferent to Zhorzhik's worsening health, but her overwhelming desire for possessions blinds her to everything else. Only at odd moments does she realize the danger to Zhorzhik, and then she quickly brushes aside her fears: " 'Absolutely nothing will happen to him,' shouted Shurka with deliberate rudeness . . . 'I'll fix him up here better than any hospital. I'll fry cutlets for him and he can eat as much as he wants!' But once again a coldness stole around her heart" (I, 365).

The story of Zhorzhik and Shurka is a satirical comedy, but—unlike most of Kataev's satirical sketches and stories—it has its tragic side and is based on character rather than situation. The theme of obsession with material wealth clearly touches a chord in the author himself, enabling him to see beyond the humorous side of human imperfection and to hint at tragedy beneath the amusing surface of "Things."

V   The Embezzlers

If in 1924 and the early part of 1925 adventure novels about death rays and secret passages were topical, then in the second half of 1925 and through into 1927 the theme of embezzlement gripped the imagination of several writers as reflecting an aspect of life in the NEP period.[17] The subject of *The Embezzlers* is the theft of a large sum by two petty officials—an accountant named Filipp Stepanovich Prokhorov, and his cashier, Vanechka.[18] Following a spate of thefts from other offices, the accountant and cashier are actually expected to abscond with their firm's money. Quite by accident (and partly through the suggestions of a fellow worker), they get drunk and find themselves on a train to Leningrad with a huge sum. There follows a round of drunken encounters with various swindlers, intent on parting the embezzlers from their cash. From Leningrad they travel to a provincial town and a village, and then on to the South, and everywhere they go there is vodka to sustain their dream. Finally, with all their money spent, they realize what they have done and return to face retribution.

The inspiration for *The Embezzlers* came when Kataev was sent to the provincial town of Tver, where there had been a number of cases of embezzlement. He was struck, above all, by the way in which the NEP period had revived the old instinct for enrichment, as if the Revolution, Civil War, and period of War Communism were but a temporary episode: "Suddenly, in a working-class town, there were embezzlers. After [the slogan] 'peace to the huts, war to the palaces,' there were again people maddened by the desire to grab something for themselves, just as in the old days."[19]

The magnificent opening passage of *The Embezzlers* establishes this basic theme. The Russia of the NEP period may aspire to being a new society, but in fact it has not changed since Gogol's days. In Moscow the former Myasnitskaya Street may have been renamed First of May Street, but that does not mean it is in any way different:

But who could bring himself to call it that in the middle of November, at that dreary hour of the morning when the fine Moscow drizzle tiresomely and unremittingly soaks the passersby, when incredibly long rods of uncertain function, clanging away on a cart which is turning a corner, manage to hit you in the face with their sharp ends, when your way is suddenly barred by a milling machine or a dynamo spilling out of some engineering office straight across the pavement, when a great cart horse thumps you on the shoulder with the iron-covered shaft of its cart, and the wheel of a car sends a great wave of mud over your already bespattered coat, when the glass signs of finance companies stun you with their sinister gold letters, when millstones, chaff-cutters, saws and gear mechanisms are ready to leap from their place at any moment, smashing through the gloomy shop windows, throw themselves at you and make mincemeat of you, when at every corner there's a smell of lamp gas from a broken pipe, when green lamps burn all day above office-workers' desks—when all this is happening, who could bring himself to call this street by any other name?[III, 7–8]

A change of name has not altered the street's fundamental character. It may bear the trappings of modern technology, but it remains the same old Myasnitskaya Street, and in this sense it symbolizes Moscow and the whole of Russia in the NEP period. The inhabitants, too, remain the same as before; the new era of socialism has not changed them.

In view of this theme it is entirely appropriate that Kataev should have found a model for the syntax and intonation of this descriptive passage in the work of Gogol, who, of all Russian writers, best captured the drabness and pettiness of man's existence. This stylistic reference to the great nineteenth-century author is the first of many such in *The Embezzlers*. In particular, Kataev imitates Gogol's abundant use of whimsical comic detail. Like Akaky Akakievich, the hero of Gogol's "The Overcoat," Kataev's mild cashier delights in his repetitive, undemanding work. He reads the sign on his window from the inside as ASSAK instead of KASSA (Cashier); he enjoys making ticks with his pencil, and even gives names to inanimate objects such as his beloved pencil: "He loved his fine big pencil which was always kept really sharp. Half of it was red and the other half blue, and to himself he even called it respectfully Alexander Sidorovich—Alexander for the red half and Sidorovich for the blue" (III, 14). In the town of Kalinov, Filipp Stepanovich and Vanechka buy from a peasant a cow with markings on its side like a map of Australia. The peasant from whom they buy the cow is so amazed by the speed of the transaction that, like one of his counterparts in *Dead Souls*, he stands in the street for a long time, staring after the visitors from the capital. Or again, the main square in Kalinov is called "Former Dedushkin Square," because the chief-of-police after whom it was named was arrested for theft, and the inhabitants could not scrap a perfectly good nameplate, so they added the word "former" before the name of the disgraced official. One such comic detail comes straight from the pages of *Dead Souls* and is acknowledged as Gogolian by Kataev. While they are in Kalinov, Filipp Stepanovich and Vanechka make inquiries about the village of Berezovka, and the old man whom they ask gets confused about Berezovka and Upper Berezovka "almost like something out of Gogol." (The reference is to the confusion in *Dead Souls* between the villages of Manilovka and Zamanilovka.)

If *Dead Souls* inspires the provincial scenes of *The Embezzlers*, then Gogol's "Nevsky Prospekt" provides the model for the Leningrad scenes, in which Kataev presents a mysterious, unreal city like Gogol's St. Petersburg: "Leningrad was entirely swallowed up by an extremely dense, cold, choking fog. It was as if no city had ever really existed. As if it had appeared for a moment when they were drunk, with all its diabolic temptations and beauties, and had disappeared for ever" (III, 86).

The reference to "Nevsky Prospekt" may well have more than stylistic significance. The hero of that tale—the dreamer and artist Piskarev—is destroyed by his inability to accept the gulf between his ideals and reality. In part, Kataev parodies this situation. Instead of Gogol's idealistic artist, Kataev has an accountant whose romantic dreams about a fictitious Count Gvido form part of his social snobbery. For a while in Leningrad he becomes a member of the aristocratic circle he had long dreamed of, dispensing hospitality like a prince or a count. Whereas Piskarev's error is due to his fine, idealistic nature, Prokhorov's is due to vanity, stupidity, and drunkenness, and the result is comic rather than tragic. He is deceived by Leningrad not because "the devil has lit the lamps," as in Gogol's story, but because of his own vulgar ambitions and gullibility.

The links between *The Embezzlers* and Gogol's work are of great importance. First, Kataev's ability to mimic style allows him to create a comic and whimsical atmosphere in the Gogolian manner which proves an ideal medium for his satirical tale. Second, the references to Gogol serve as a constant reminder that the author's major intention is to show the features of an older Russia, known to the nineteenth-century writer, forcing their way through the veneer of Soviet reality.

Despite one or two voices raised to the contrary, it is now generally acknowledged that *The Embezzlers* played an important part in the development of the Soviet satirical novel.[20] In particular, two famous works—*The Twelve Chairs* (1928) and *The Golden Calf* (1931)—by Ilf and Petrov follow the pattern established by Kataev of a picaresque novel with satirical pictures of life in the NEP and post-NEP period.[21] Satire in *The Embezzlers* is aimed at two main (and closely related) targets: first, the survival into the Soviet period of customs and social attitudes which should have perished with the old regime; and second, various negative aspects of Soviet society under NEP, ranging from bureaucracy to alcoholism.

The survival of bourgeois social attitudes into the Soviet period is most clearly seen in the figure of the novel's central character,

Filipp Stepanovich Prokhorov. His very first appearance provides a hint that Filipp Stepanovich harbors social ambitions: he is described as "an extremely respectable middle-aged gentleman wearing goloshes, a thick overcoat with an astrakhan collar, and an astrakhan pork-pie hat with an upturned brim and an astrakhan band" (III, 7). As with Gogol, the author's protestations that his character is "extremely respectable" somehow suggest the opposite. And the abundance of astrakhan points to Filipp Stepanovich's sense of his own importance, which soon emerges explicitly. While at work he would sometimes daydream that "he was none other than an experienced general standing on a promontory and controlling with courage and subtlety some exceptionally complex military operations" (III, 11–12). In his imagination his own modest exploits during the Russo-Japanese War become exaggerated, as, for example, when he places an advertisement in the Moscow *Marriage Gazette* in which he describes himself as "a warrior, a decorated hero of Port Arthur . . . a Son of Mars" (III, 12).

In a comic detail that is Gogolian in its absurdity, Kataev suggests that Filipp Stepanovich's desire to belong to the aristocray and his sense of superiority to ordinary people may have arisen from a line in a novel which he once read. "It is quite possible that it arose many years before, at that precise moment when Filipp Stepanovich, on guard duty near Chemulpo, lay on his stomach in a sorghum field and read the following illustrious line from a high society novel: 'Count Gvido jumped on his horse . . .' " (III, 13). He soon forgets the novel, but that single phrase imprints itself on his memory, and he sometimes imagines himself to be Count Gvido.[22]

One of Filipp Stepanovich's heroes is, then, a fictitious aristocrat; the other is a successful businessman, old Mr. Sabbakin, who owned the company for which the accountant worked before the Revolution. Whenever he has to deal with a novel situation—especially one involving social behavior—Filipp Stepanovich tries to act as old Mr. Sabbakin would have. For example, when he orders a meal in a restaurant he recalls the panache with which his former employer used to do this and tries to imitate it.

Having taken care to depict Filipp Stepanovich as a man with almost boundless respect for the great ones of the old regime—the aristocrats and capitalists—Kataev then introduces his character into an aristocratic milieu in one of the most memorable scenes in the whole of his work. The former aristocrats of St. Petersburg, who

have fallen on hard times since the Revolution, have gathered together to work as extras on a film set. (The public has an un-
quenchable thirst for films about the great ones.) After the film has
been shot, a "well-known crook called Zhorzhik" realizes that there
is profit to be made from keeping the group together to satisfy the
curiosity and vanity of tourists anxious to mix in high society. In
order to make an even greater impression on his customers, Zhorzhik retains the services of the man who played Tsar Nicholas in
the film, a baker called Sereda ("Mr. Average") who happens to be
"the spitting image of the late Tsar."

In the presentation of the "Tsar" and the aristocrats Kataev employs a device which he had used in "Sir Henry and the Devil" and
to which he was to return in *Time, Forward!*, namely the development without comment of a situation that is absurd or incomprehensible, followed by an explanation that resolves the mystery.
Thus, the "Tsar" and his entourage are first seen through the eyes
of the drunken embezzlers, who want to believe in the existence
of the Tsar and the splendor of the aristocracy. The reader knows
that Tsar Nicholas could not really be living in Leningrad in the
mid 1920s, yet only later does the author provide the explanation
involving the baker who looks like Nicholas.[23] As a result, although
the description is perfectly realistic, it produces an effect of grotesque unreality (the more so since the author allows his own viewpoint to intrude in one detail, by referring to the Tsar throughout
the passage as "the late Emperor Nicholas"). By presenting this
scene and others through the eyes of his drunken heroes, Kataev
introduces into the style of the work an element of fantasy similar
to that produced by delirium in "Sir Henry and the Devil." Nothing
is certain to remain completely stable; sudden shifts of perception
and strange perspectives abound as the two embezzlers float in the
half-real world of drunkenness. The use of abrupt transformations
and unusual angles of vision links Kataev closely to other Soviet
authors of the 1920s like Yury Olesha and Veniamin Kaverin, who
were experimenting in a similar fashion.[24]

The satirical importance of the drunken viewpoint lies in the
switch from the fantasy which it creates to a prosaic and sordid
reality. For example, Vanechka (who shares some of his colleague's
social ambition) longs to meet a real countess, and his wish is
granted. In the setting of the large house where he first sees her
she appears alluring, with her Persian shawl, her crossed legs, and

her oriental eyes. But on reaching her home he discovers that she is nothing more than a prostitute who lives in indescribable squalor. Once again Kataev has turned "Nevsky Prospekt" upside down, for where, in Gogol's tale, a prostitute is mistaken for a princess by the idealistic hero, in the later work a real princess turns out to be a prostitute. The shock to Vanechka is so great that for a moment he obtains insight into what he looks like and what he has done, and a note of real pathos complicates the book's comic tone (anticipating its final chapters). One critic has observed that the episode with the aristocrats shows that only in a drunken stupor can the old world be raised again.[25] This is partly true, but it does not go far enough. The romantic dreams of the two embezzlers obscure the reality of high society no less than their drunkenness. The snobbery of people like Filipp Stepanovich, whom the Revolution has altered not one whit, enables the old world to continue to exist.

For this, the first of the targets for Kataev's satire, his main satirical methods (the contrasts between drunken and sober viewpoints and frequent references to the style of Gogol) prove very apt, for they both serve to emphasize the artificiality of the embezzlers' dreams.

Yet although the fantasies of Filipp Stepanovich and Vanechka are exposed for what they are, the real world in which they find themselves is, for the most part, one from which it is desirable to escape into dreams, and herein lies Kataev's second satirical target (and also, incidentally, the reason for the sympathy which the heroes evoke). The encounters with the prostitute in the grotesquely (and no doubt misleadingly!) named "Hotel Hygienic" and with a roguish book salesman illustrate an important aspect of life in Russia during the NEP period, and of satirical literature of the time: the power of money and the opportunism of grasping people. The city to which the innocent embezzlers come is as grotesque a place as ever Gogol created, for it is a city inhabited, apparently exclusively, by rogues, prostitutes, and confidence tricksters ready to prey on such naive newcomers as Filipp Stepanovich and Vanechka. Yet although Kataev satirizes this aspect of NEP Russia, his censure of those who have adapted to new conditions and who continue to make money by trickery is not severe. The book salesman has the same sort of appeal as Ostap Bender, the opportunistic hero of Ilf and Petrov's novels. Kataev's sympathy for this type of clever rogue permeates the entire characterization.

If everyone in Leningrad appears to be looking for an easy way to make money, then everyone in all of Russia appears to crave vodka desperately. The second aspect of NEP Russia satirized by Kataev is alcoholism. Besides the embezzlers themselves, many other characters seem to spend much of their time drinking. Yet once again, although his picture of provincial life is very depressing, Kataev's attitude appears to be one of sardonic amusement mixed with a certain sympathy rather than of severe censure, for only vodka can dispel the gloom, boredom, and terrible drabness of life. When the heroes first arrive in Kalinov they are depressed by the sight of its cheerless gray streets, broken-down buildings, and sub-dued inhabitants. But by the time they return from their brief visit to Vanechka's home village, vodka has come on sale, and the town has undergone a complete transformation: "The town of Kalinov was unrecognizable. What had happened to the former air of bore-dom? Lights blazed in the windows of the inns and the wine shops. Crowds of people stood outside . . . On all sides could be heard harmonicas and balalaikas. The streets and alleys were full of the local good-for-nothings, staggering about in groups or on their own, drunk as lords" (III, 109–10). At least with vodka on sale the town shakes off the stultifying boredom and lethargy which grip its in-habitants when they are sober.

In similar fashion vodka releases Filipp Stepanovich from the crushing boredom of his life and allows him to indulge his sweet dreams. In a sense, the embezzlement and the (albeit illusory) freedom which it brings correspond to the liberating, intoxicating effect of alcohol. The embezzlers' crime contains a large element of wish fulfillment. It answers the question "what if?" "What if there were no restraints?" "What if we could travel now away from this dreary place?" Thus, it is entirely appropriate that their orgy of wish fulfillment should be carried out in an almost perpetual state of drunkenness.

In this discussion of the influence of Gogol and the elements of satire in *The Embezzlers* it has been necessary to consider the major characteristics of Filipp Stepanovich and Vanechka, but some fur-ther comments must be made.

Throughout the novel the embezzlers remain entirely passive. They commit the act of theft because their colleague Nikita is so afraid that they will abscond with the money before he receives his wages that he accompanies them to the bank and then to the restaurant where they first get drunk. The simple Nikita takes on a demonic aspect in the eyes of the embezzlers as he goes with them to the station and sees them onto the train. His will appears to dominate them in the entire opening episode, and that sets the pattern for future encounters; for most of the characters whom they meet on their travels manipulate the passive and essentially innocent embezzlers. In the hands of another author, Nikita's transformation into a demonic creature might have been of great psychological importance, for the scene has a superficially Dostoevskian quality. But Kataev turns it into a joke at the expense of his embezzlers and at the cliché of the almost supernatural force of will.

Though they indulge in an act of wild abandon, the embezzlers remain true to their callings as accountant and cashier. Filipp Stepanovich authorizes Vanechka to pay for goods or services just as if they were still at their desks in Moscow:

Filipp Stepanovich examined the tickets thoroughly and gave them to Vanechka. "Vanechka, file these vouchers," he said in the same relaxed and calm business-like tone in which he usually addressed his subordinates in the office. And suddenly it seemed to him that his whole journey was a high-level official business trip of great governmental importance. [III, 44]

For most of its length *The Embezzlers* remains a comic stylization of NEP-period Russia. Its characters are grotesquely one-sided (the hint of psychological depth proves illusory), but because they move in a grotesque world there is no sense of jarring incongruity. As Viktor Shklovsky puts it: "*The Embezzlers* is like a fish on a mirror. It is impossible to dive into that brilliant surface."[26] Kataev does not try to portray characters in the round, or to present a balanced, realistic picture of life in Russia. His concern is with surface brilliance, not with depths of feeling and motivation. *The Embezzlers* presents a striking picture of one side of Russian life as it appears to an amused and detached observer. However, in the final chapters Kataev attempts to introduce another view of Russia, to set his stylized heroes in a realistic context in order to reveal the distortion of reality by a change of focus. In the chapter in which Vanechka meets his mother the tone becomes serious and pathetic:

The mistress of the house broke out in red blotches. She suddenly understood why Vanechka had come from the city, why he had money, and who

Filipp Stepanovich was. Everything was as clear as daylight. And to think she had been glad! Her son would stay at home a while, she had thought. He would go to Grusha's wedding, and perhaps stay altogether and look after the farm. Things were different with a man around the place. And it turns out like this! She was so ashamed she couldn't even look people in the eye. [III, 105]

The intention behind such passages may be evident enough, but the fact remains that their pathetic tone jars slightly with the novel's prevailing atmosphere. The attempt to humanize the Bashmachkin-like Vanechka by giving him a solid home background strikes a discordant note. In the final chapter both embezzlers wake from their dreamlike state and reenter the normal, realistic world in which they must undergo punishment for their crime. The pathos with which the author tries to invest them at this point seems misplaced after his earlier superficial portraits. "Five years! And he began to think about that wonderful, remarkable, and inevitable day in five years' time when he would come out of prison to freedom" (III, 128).

Just as the opening chapter contains a long street description, so does the final one, thereby enclosing the novel in a frame. But the two descriptions differ greatly in tone. Instead of a drab November day on which everything appeared depressing, the final scene takes place on a fine, frosty March day, with a corresponding change in the mood of the city.

The sun was setting behind the blue roofs. The pink, completely cloudless sky lay soft and beautiful beyond the cupolas of the Strastnoy Monastery. Hoarfrost fell from the white branches along the avenue. The firm snow crunched and squeaked like saltpeter underfoot. Some caretakers were clearing snow from the roof of a tile-fronted five-story house. Solid layers of it flew out from the eaves at a dizzy height into the blue smoke and, getting bigger and bigger, hurtled downwards like compact rolls of white cloth, unwinding on the way like undulating bolts of cambric and disintegrating with a smack at the foot of the house . . . The very thin sickle of the moon had appeared over the town and a man in an Austrian greatcoat was already setting up his telescope near the Pushkin monument. Clusters of balloons—red, blue, and green—floated above the crowd, swaying and squeaking against one another, gladdening the eye with their brightness like a magic-lantern show or a child's colored transfer. The city breathed the young breath of feet and wheels. [III, 127]

Kataev's change of focus which allows the reader to see past the artificial world of the embezzlers to a very different one where honest people work soberly corresponds on a larger scale to the device used elsewhere in the book of contrasting a distorted view of something with an undistorted view. But there is no doubt that it is the seedy Russia the embezzlers encounter in the course of their adventures rather than the healthy, hard-working land of the final chapter that holds the author's interest.

In *The Embezzlers* several features of Kataev's work of the 1920s combine to form a mature and satisfying novel. The sharp sense of humor, the portrayal of unusual states of mind, the love of parody and stylization, the ambiguous attitude toward those who have adapted to Soviet society and who continue to survive through opportunism—all of these are common aspects of Kataev's work in this decade. Above all, perhaps, the mixture of realism and fantasy, of sober, of accurate descriptions with unusual distortions and associations, marks *The Embezzlers* as the work of the mature Kataev. Not until the 1960s was such a blend to recur in his work to any extent.

VI   *Drama*

The Moscow Art Theater's production of *The Embezzlers* may have been a failure, as discussed in Chapter 1, but for Kataev it proved to be the beginning of a short creative period as a dramatist. His best plays were all written between 1927 and 1933.

Squaring the Circle, written in 1927, achieved great success both in the Soviet Union and abroad. The play is a light-hearted comedy in which two young couples, forced by the housing shortage to share a room, discover that they have made the wrong choice of partner, and after several misunderstandings eventually exchange spouses. Three of the young people are members of the Komsomol—the Young Communist League—and some of the humor derives from their use of current Communist jargon, but essentially the play is too good-humored to be satirical at the expense of either the Komsomol or the acute housing shortage. It owes more to the traditional French farce than to its contemporary setting among Komsomol students. According to one reviewer, the first production at the Moscow Satire Theater failed because the director emphasized the "problems" posed by the play rather than its humor. In the Moscow

Art Theater production Nikolay Gorchakov stressed that the play was above all a joke and must be played accordingly.[27]

Squaring the Circle exhibits several features of Kataev's humorous and satirical prose works of the 1920s, so much so that it may be considered a development in a different genre of his sketches and stories. The situation that serves as a plot is anecdotal—recalling the many everyday situations in the sketches—and is exploited for its inherent humor rather than for any satirical point. Within the larger framework of a full-length play, Kataev develops character more than he can in a short sketch, but his four young people remain types rather than individuals. In its details, too, the play echoes or anticipates prose works of the 1920s. For example, the shortage of living space forms part of the plot of "Eduard the Loafer" and "The Child"; the love affair between Vanya and Tonya (recalled in Act I, Scene 13) resembles in detail that described in the story "In Winter"; the use by Abram and Tonya of Party jargon in incongruous situations recalls a similar feature of *The Embezzlers* (where the jargon had been bureaucratic rather than Party).

All these examples illustrate the close links between *Squaring the Circle* and Kataev's prose works of the 1920s, both satirical and nonsatirical. But, as almost always with Kataev, it is necessary to take a broader view, to see what was being written by other authors at this time in order to assess the influences on the play. The two subjects of *Squaring the Circle*—the sexual morality of Komsomol members and the extreme shortage of living space—were popular themes in the press and in literature at this time.[28] The former theme, in particular, inspired such controversial works as Pantaleymon Romanov's "Without Cherry Blossom" and Sergey Malashkin's "The Moon from the Right Side" (both 1926). Kataev's approach to the "problem" of sex, marriage, and morality is indicated by an incident in Act II, Scene 3, in which Abram and Tonya use two pages of "The Moon from the Right Side" to wrap sausage. Abram frequently agonizes over whether his actions are "ethical," though he does not restrict this question to matters of sexual morality, but also applies it to petty acts such as taking a slice of his room-mate's sausage. In this way Kataev derided the ethical dilemmas posed in many contemporary works.

The play's most remarkable feature is its simplicity. Only the four central characters have significant roles, and the basic method involves repetition and near-repetition. Almost every scene involving two of the characters corresponds to a scene involving the other two, and often the dialogue is repeated with only minor variations. The author treats all four characters with equal warmth and gentle irony—Lyudmila, the rather vulgar practical girl; Tonya, the idealistic, impractical Komsomol member; Vanya, the lively, stylish extrovert; and Abram, the quiet, thoughtful Komsomol. Kataev sympathizes with all four and laughs at all four in equal measure.

It is not possible within the confines of the present book to discuss in detail Kataev's next two plays, written in the early 1930s, *Million terzanii (A Million Torments)* and *Doroga tsvetov (The Flowery Path)*, but it is worth noting that they share a much harsher satirical tone, being directed against the posturing of pseudo-intellectuals. The critics were very hard on these plays, and especially on their "one-sided picture of Soviet society."[29] In the 1930s, when literature came to be regarded as a tool in the struggle to build a modern industrial society, it was increasingly difficult to write and publish satire. Ilf and Petrov's *The Golden Calf*, for instance, was only published after a great effort by Gorky to have it accepted.[30] As the 1930s progressed, criticism of Soviet society, with whatever intention, could no longer be tolerated and had to be replaced by positive support. For Kataev this meant the end of the satirical genre as such, except for sketches aimed against foreigners. And although he did paint occasional satirical portraits in later novels, only in the 1960s did satire reemerge as a significant element in his work.

VII *Criticism of Kataev's Work of the 1920s*

The earliest significant review of Kataev's work appeared in 1925 and dealt with the collection of stories entitled *Bezdel'nik Eduard (Eduard the Loafer)*.[31] The reviewer is more impressed by Kataev's technical skill (which he relates to the art of the cinema) than by the content of his stories, and views the heroes of the Civil War stories as anti-Soviet but impotent members of the intelligentsia. There is no suggestion, however, that such negative characters should be excluded from Soviet literature. On the contrary, the reviewer gives a guarded welcome to a new talent.

The Embezzlers also met with an enthusiastic response from critics. All the principal reviewers accepted the notion that the Russia portrayed by Kataev is not a photographic reproduction of the real

Russia, but a stylized country where certain negative features have been exaggerated.[32] One interesting review distinguishes between Kataev's point of view and that of his heroes.[33] But critics of a slightly later period—the early 1930s—rejected such a distinction and attacked Kataev for his one-sided representation of Russia in *The Embezzlers*.[34]

In September and November 1930 a two-part article criticizing Kataev in the most severe terms appeared in the RAPP journal *Na literaturnom postu (On Literary Guard)*. Its author, Iosif Mashbits-Verov, reviewed the entire corpus of Kataev's work of the 1920s and, while admitting that it had some merit (notably the sharp observation, the wit, and the sophisticated style), he found that on the whole Kataev had exerted a negative influence on Soviet literature. The critic's central point appears in a brief paragraph near the beginning of his article: "Kataev does not seek to make his readers struggle; on the contrary, he seeks (possibly unconsciously) to make them 'mere existers,' so to speak, thoughtless 'enjoyers' of life."[35] An analysis of the underlying philosophy of stories such as "The Father" leads the critic to the conclusion that for Kataev all of life is beautiful, irrespective of social conditions; the important things are love and art. He then goes on to discuss critically both Kataev's portrayal of revolutionaries and his humor. Of *The Embezzlers*, Mashbits-Verov says that Kataev's superficial philosophy leads him to turn a serious social problem into a joke.

Finally, Mashbits-Verov poses some threatening questions about Kataev's future. "The basic question is this: how should one react to Kataev's work? Is he an enemy or an artist who can be 'transformed,' changed, 'won over' to the side of the Revolution?"[36] He suggests that Kataev, though not yet an enemy of the Soviet regime, is on the very brink of becoming one.[37]

Mashbits-Verov's article was part of a campaign against fellow-travelers by RAPP and other left-wing critics in the late 1920s and early 1930s, when more and more frequently authors were exhorted to "transform themselves" into active supporters of the regime.[38] There can be little doubt that such external pressure played a great part in Kataev's change of direction in the 1930s, although one cannot entirely dismiss the desire to respond to the overall atmosphere of concerted effort in that decade as a factor in his "transformation." Whatever the balance between external pressure to change and a desire to remain topical and publish without too much censure, the fact remains that with the coming of the 1930s Kataev ceased to be a fellow-traveler, altered his themes and his manner of writing, and entered upon a new phase of his career.

CHAPTER 4

"Writing Like Walter Scott"

IN her memoirs Nadezhda Mandelshtam recalls that, besides the terror which hung in the air as a constant threat, the period of the 1930s was one in which rich material rewards were available in return for conformity, a price which all but the most exceptional writers were prepared to pay. She writes: "The new Moscow was now being built up and adopting the ways of the world—people were opening their first bank accounts, buying furniture, and writing novels. Everybody could hope for speedy advancement because every day somebody was plucked from their midst and had to be replaced."[1] Like most prose writers of his generation, faced with the open threats of critics, Kataev tried to secure for himself some of the privileges which were now at hand. Nadezhda Mandelshtam quotes him as saying: "Nowadays one must write like Walter Scott."[2] But his works of the 1930s cannot be lightly dismissed as hack work. Their relatively high artistic standard testifies to his talent and his desire to keep himself attuned to the spirit of the age.

Each of Kataev's longer works of this period reflects the precise time when it was written. All three share an element of active support for the regime which distinguishes them from earlier works, but they are not a homogeneous group, and the differences between them illustrate some of the major trends in Soviet literature of the 1930s. *Time, Forward!* captures the heady atmosphere of socialist competition during the first Five Year Plan early in the decade; *Lone White Sail* is both a historical novel and a work for children (two popular genres from the mid-1930s onward); and *I, a Son of the Working People* deals through the medium of recent history with the threat of a future war against Germany. Thus, the sense of topicality which Kataev had shown in the 1920s remains a feature of his work in the next decade.

I Time, Forward!

Kataev arrived in Magnitogorsk in May 1931 in time to witness an attempt by a brigade of shock-workers to lay a record number

of mixes of concrete in an eight-hour shift. On May 29 the brigadier
and his men laid 429 mixes, beating the world standard and succeeding in their socialist competition against the workers of Kuz-
netskstroy.[3] Here was a subject that struck a chord in Kataev. His
belief that socialist competition should involve "struggle, a raised
temperature, a quickened pulse, a vein standing out on the forehead" accorded with the extraordinary effort being put into completing the Magnitogorsk site.[4] He already had the title for a novel,
for he had been struck by a line from Mayakovsky's play *The Bath
House*: "Forward, o Time! Time, forward!" When he commented
to the poet that the phrase would make an excellent title for a novel,
Mayakovsky replied that he did not write novels and that if Kataev
wanted to use the line, he could.[5]

The story of the attempt by a brigade of construction workers to
beat the world record for the number of concrete mixes in a shift
might not seem very promising material for a novel. Yet Kataev
manages to sustain the pace and to limit the time span to the one
day of the record attempt, with no substantial flashbacks to provide
background details.[6] He accomplishes this by taking a large number
of characters through the day, and switching frequently from one
subplot to another. Thus, there are two main elements in the novel's
construction: a temporal element which gives the work overall unity,
and a number of subplots involving characters of different nationalities and social classes which accounts for its diversity.

Though Kataev originally intended to cover the work of all three
shifts during the day in question, he finally concentrated on the
middle one worked by Ishchenko's brigade.[7] However, although
the other two shifts diminished in importance, the three-part structure of the original conception corresponded to setting, main action,
and denouement, and this tripartite structure is retained. In chapters 2–41 Kataev sets the scene, introducing all of the characters
and situations. (Chapter 1 is postponed until near the end of the
novel for reasons to be discussed below.) In comparison with the
feverish activity of the middle section (chapters 42–61), devoted to
Ishchenko's shift, the pace of the long introduction is leisurely. One
reviewer compared Kataev's technique in the early part of the novel
to a fan which is opened out further and further, but which is still
held together at the base and so can be neatly gathered in again.[8]
The long, diverse introduction proves essential, for once the main
action begins there is no time for character or situation development.

The second section is devoted almost entirely to action, to the many difficulties met and overcome in the record attempt. Here Kataev utilizes familiar devices of the adventure novel—the temporary defection of a member of the brigade, the storm which adds to the difficulties, the injury which seems likely to end the bid altogether, the sudden arrival of reinforcements from an unexpected quarter.

Finally, the later chapters, as well as the transposed first chapter, serve as a denouement. Those situations which have been interrupted by the main action—for example, Fenya's childbearing and Klava's journey away from Magnitogorsk—are resolved as the day draws to its close. The first chapter occupies a penultimate position partly as a striking device to emphasize the novel's theme of man outstripping time, and partly because it presents the result of the quality tests carried out on the concrete a week after it has been laid (i.e., outside the single day of the action).

Turning now to the second constructional element, we see that the extreme concentration of time is balanced by an expansive treatment of space. The narrative appears to deal with only one sector of one construction site, but that sector in fact stands for the whole country. As Kataev puts it in his letter to Alexander Smolyan in Chapter 1: "You taught me to see a garden in a raindrop" (III, 425). The activity in one small corner of the land reflects what is happening elsewhere. For instance, Magnitogorsk resembles the front line in a battle—its cement-mixers standing like howitzers, the ground torn up as if by shellfire; but at the rear, in Moscow, the battle is also being waged. There, too, streets become unrecognizable as demolition and reconstruction daily alter the face of the city. For the scenes set in Moscow Kataev drew heavily on an article which he had written in 1930 presenting a vivid picture of the modernization of the capital: "The general reconstruction of the streets had temporarily transformed Moscow into a hell. The tram and bus routes altered every day, every hour."[9] These lines from the article go almost unaltered into the novel (III, 221), as does the memorable description of a diver with which the article ends.[10]

Just as Kataev handles time so as to suggest man's struggle to defeat it, "to get ahead of it," so also does he emphasize man's technological victory over space. Magnitogorsk and Moscow may be far apart, but they are engaged in an identical war, and are helped by modern technology such as the telephone, which brings them close together. When Margulies enters a telephone booth to speak to his sister in Moscow, he seems to stop the flow of time by isolating himself from the events around him, but he becomes aware of space: "As soon as he placed the receiver to his ear, space spoke in place of halted time. It spoke through the near and distant voices of operators, through the faint crackle of atmospherics, through the roar of the rushing kilometers, through the mosquito hum of signals, through the exchange of messages between cities" (III, 195).

The parallels between Moscow and Magnitogorsk form one major aspect of Kataev's handling of space; the other consists of Magnitogorsk's role as a microcosm of the entire Soviet Union. Here all the nationalities which inhabit that vast land are represented among the tens of thousands of workers. "There came dignified people from Kostroma, with slightly distended nostrils; there came Tartars from Kazan; Georgians and Chechens from the Caucasus; there came Bashkirs, Germans, Muscovities, Leningraders in jackets and Russian blouses; there came Ukrainians, Jews, Belorussians" (III, 192). The characters in the foreground reflect the ethnic mutiplicity of this vast mass of workers: Margulies is a Jew, Zagirov a Tartar, Ishchenko a Ukrainian, Khanumov an Uzbek, Klava a Russian.

Similarly, construction work is not the only activity at Magnitogorsk (and, by extension, elsewhere in the country). Forming the background to the work of the concrete-layers is an extensive picture of life in the town. People prepare and sell meals; they sell books and newspapers; nurses attend to pregnant women in labor; long lines form outside the barber shop; workers rehearse a play after hours; there is even a menagerie with an elephant which escapes at the height of the storm.

Common to both elements of of the construction—time and space—is the influence of the cinema. In an article of 1936 about the effects of the cinema on authors of his generation Kataev writes: "The elements of cinematic montage—the very concept of *montage*—became for many authors of my generation an integral concept in our work."[11] He goes on to discuss briefly the influence of the cinema on *Erendorf Island*, *The Embezzlers*, and *Time, Forward!*, the last of which he characterizes as having been "constructed literally on cinematic principles."[12] The concept of montage does, indeed, help to elucidate the construction of *Time, Forward!*, which in a way resembles the highly cinematic work of Arthur Hailey. The many short scenes; the "cutting" from one scene to the next; the lack of background information about characters; the way in which the author's eye sweeps and tracks like a camera in his landscape descriptions—all of these techniques of *Time, Forward!* testify to the influence of the cinema upon it.

It is a remarkable feature of *Time, Forward!* that, although it marks the beginning of Kataev's committed writing, each issue is presented from at least two points of view. Few if any arguments remain uncontradicted, and while, in the end, the novel's message emerges plainly, Kataev's own former sympathies are still detectible. In accordance with this pattern of polyphony, the characters divide into groups, consisting mostly of antithetical figures, all of whom are more or less one-sided.

Many of the major characters are identified by a physical feature or idiosyncrasy used as a leitmotif. Thus, Korneev worries about the state of his shoes, and affects a strange pronunciation of the word for "mix"; Margulies eats boiled sweets; Shura Soldatova has outgrown her girlish clothes. In this way the principal figures can be readily identified by the reader, and an aspect of their character is suggested through the recurring detail. The use of physical rather than psychological details in characterization is, of course, typical of Kataev.

Appropriately enough in a novel about building, the conflict on which the action rests occurs between two engineers: the audacious and inspiring Margulies, and the cautious and ultimately reactionary Nalbandov. Associated with the two engineers are two slogans encapsulating their views. "Two ideas—'construction work is not a stunt' and 'in an age of reconstruction the rate of work is all-important'—began to struggle with each other, and the signs of this incipient struggle followed Nalbandov everywhere" (III, 263).

Superficially, the quarrel between Margulies and Nalbandov involves technical engineering policy, but the attitudes expressed by the two slogans have far wider implications for the future of Soviet society. Nalbandov believes that the pace of work should not be so high as to endanger the valuable imported machinery. For him, construction work is not a sporting event with records to be broken. This appears to be a reasonable view, but against it (and in favor of Margulies's desire for increased pace) Kataev pits no less an authority than Stalin. Twice in *Time, Forward!* Kataev quotes directly from a speech of Stalin's about the need to industrialize rapidly in order to stave off the danger of a military disaster, such as had plagued Russia for centuries.

"Not to increase the pace of work means to fall behind. And those who fall behind are beaten. But we do not want to be beaten. No, we will not have that! The history of old Russia consisted in being constantly beaten because she was backward. She was beaten by the Mongol khans. She was beaten by the Turkish beks. She was beaten by the Swedish feudal lords. She was beaten by the Polish and Lithuanian gentry. She was beaten by the English and French capitalists. She was beaten by the Japanese barons. She was beaten by everyone, because of her backwardness. Because of military backwardness, because of cultural backwardness, because of governmental backwardness, because of industrial backwardness, because of agricultural backwardness. She was beaten because it was profitable to do so, and it went unpunished . . . "
"That is why we can no longer be backward. . . . "[13]

In the light of such a speech from such a source Nalbandov's reasonableness places him in the same category as the more blatant saboteurs who play such an important part in Soviet novels of this period.

Margulies is the novel's positive hero. As in the case of Levinson, the hero of Alexander Fadeev's *The Rout*, Margulies's biography emerges only after his tasks have been completed; private life is subordinated to public life. His devotion to duty is such that he foregoes sleep and food in order to work. He gets up before the alarm rings because "he could not trust such a precious thing as time to such a basically simple mechanism as a clock" (III, 131). His desire for greater pace is not reckless, for he bases his record attempt on the latest technical information obtained over the telephone from Moscow; but while his enthusiasm is held in check by common sense, he will not let events proceed at their normal pace. If technology can be used to speed things up, Margulies will resort to it. Herein lies the principal difference between Margulies and Kataev's earlier heroes. Almost without exception, the latter were passive, detached people, prepared to accept whatever life brought. Margulies, on the other hand, shapes his own life and the lives of others, even to the extent of challenging time and nature.

Like most positive heroes in Soviet literature, Margulies remains unidimensional. Kataev replaces complexity with an inoffensive eccentricity, summed up in Margulies's liking for boiled sweets and his childlike wonder at the enormous scale of things in Magnitogorsk. His motivation is never questioned, and little is made of his traumatic childhood, in which his family suffered in a pogrom. Essentially, he typifies the positive, energetic hero of the first Five Year Plan period who draws his strength from his ideological conviction.

Nalbandov is the antithesis of Margulies. He strikes American visitors as a typically efficient, leather-coated Bolshevik, but in his heart he fears socialist competition, for it does not accord with his dry, controlled, bureaucratic way of life. The huge inkwell on his desk, which seems to increase in size, is used as a leitmotif for Nalbandov in the way that physical features are for other characters.

Like another, though far greater, bureaucrat in Russian literature, Alexey Karenin, Nalbandov is in fact a more interesting figure than he at first appears. His motives for opposing Margulies are complex. He genuinely fears for the machinery; and he agrees with the Americans that the town being thrown together so hastily will have neither tradition nor culture. He may be officious and bureaucratic, but he is also intelligent, cultured, and articulate, and his discomfort at having to express views that he secretly opposes interests Kataev. Yet, for the sake of ideological clarity, the author suddenly vitiates this character by turning him into a moral bankrupt. At the end Nalbandov draws up two contradictory charges against Margulies and has to choose between them, which means that he is motivated less by principle and concern for the success of Magnitogorsk than by hatred of Margulies. This sudden twist introduces a false note, but nevertheless Nalbandov must be considered one of the novel's more interesting characters.

The two leading women in *Time, Forward!* never meet, but they oppose each other as starkly as do the engineers. Indeed, the contrast between them is used as a structural device, for the train journeys which they make occur in symmetrical chapters at the beginning and end of the novel, forming a kind of frame. Significantly, the important Stalin speech is quoted in each of these chapters.

Fenya, an unsophisticated country girl, discovers she is pregnant and comes to Magnitogorsk to be reunited with the child's father, Ishchenko. She had imagined that finding him would be easy, but she gets lost among the mass of new buildings, gravel piles, foundation-pits, and barbed wire. The author depicts her with the tenderness and gentle humor he generally shows to children and unsophisticated women. (One is reminded of Polechka from "The Child.") The principal device used to convey Kataev's attitude in such cases is semidirect speech (*nesobstvenno-priamaia rech'*), an intermediary form between direct and indirect speech. The language is that which would be· used by the character, but as there are no quotation marks, the narrative appears to be coming from the author. In this way Kataev aligns himself with his character and elicits from his reader an attitude of amused sympathy toward the character.

For an unsophisticated woman like Fenya, the spirit of optimism in Magnitogorsk outweighs the disadvantages of remoteness and an unpleasant climate. But for Klava, the attractions of life in European Russia and the fear of the Magnitogorsk climate prove irresistible, and she leaves Korneev to return to her husband in Moscow. Klava shares Nalbandov's need of culture and tradition; she believes that it takes time to turn a wilderness into a real city. And so, because she refuses to accept the premise on which Magnitogorsk is being built, she must leave.

Two of the three Americans in *Time, Forward!* represent different aspects of the attitude toward Americans in Soviet literature of this period.[14] Ray Roope is a rich businessman who hates and fears the Soviet Union yet has invested in it because he cannot fail to see its potential, and is drawn to it in some fateful way. Kataev satirizes the greed and self-satisfaction which lie behind Roope's cultured facade of mildness and reason. While professing to despise modern technology—he claims it has not increased man's happiness one iota—he wallows in the comfort of a luxurious automobile and obtains his wealth from investment in industry. His own hypocrisy gives the lie to his sentimental view of man's happiness in a pre-industrial heaven. Yet, for all the absurdity of Roope's position, his views are not far removed from those advanced by more sympathetic figures in Kataev's stories of the 1920s. To Nalbandov's speech about the building of the dam Roope replies: "But why does man need all this? Water for industry. Fine. But why do we need industry? To produce goods. Fine. But why do we need goods? Are they really necessary for happiness? Youth and health alone are required for happiness" (III, 289). Also like the heroes of the 1920s, Roope has a synaesthetic fantasy about a vibrant, decadent city—a Babylon, the Odessa of the Civil War stories. "The sumptuously illuminated crowd revelled; faint sounds of music could be heard. In the distance resounded this whole powerful symphony orchestra of lights, smells, movement, passions" (III, 413). Roope shares with earlier heroes an interest in culture and an attitude of detachment from the great events of the age. But characteristics that had earlier been treated sympathetically are now satirized. Even more than Margulies, Roope illustrates Kataev's change of direction.

The other American, Thomas Bixby (or Foma Egorovich, as he is known to his Russian colleagues), is an engineer under contract to the Soviet government, who works hard in order to be able to live in comfort one day. But his mortgaging of the present to a wealthy future leads to disaster, for when he loses his savings in a bank collapse, he has no other support, and his life ceases to have any meaning.

This minor character, whose story serves to delay the main action, engages the author's sympathy and therefore is more fully realized than some of the more central figures. Kataev's by now familiar ambivalent attitude toward material wealth emerges in the touching scene where Bixby looks through a glossy magazine and dreams of owning "everything necessary for the full and absolute satisfaction of human requirements, desires, and passions" (III, 375). In the end Bixby takes an overdose of morphine and dies in a hotel fire which, in his delirium, he has started. The scene ranks among the most memorable in the book, partly because of the sympathy evoked for the character, and partly because of the striking description of the effects of the drug on Bixby's perception of the world.

Last among the leading groups of characters are the writers and journalists. The novel is dedicated to Alexander Smolyan of ROSTA, who served as one of the prototypes for the characters of Vinkich and Triger. For the important figure of the writer Georgy Vasilevich, Kataev drew on his own experiences at Magnitogorsk and those of fellow-writers who were initially confused by the immensity of the building site. Chapter 19 consists largely of random notes by Georgy Vasilevich, recording the many impressions he has registered during his first few hours on the site:

"Through my window the world opens up like a rebus. I can see a multitude of figures. People, horses, wattle carts, cables, machines, steam, letters, clouds, mountains, railway carriages, water . . . But I do not understand their interrelationship. Yet that interrelationship exists. There is some very powerful interaction. There can be no doubt about that. I know that; I believe it; but I can't see it. And that is exasperating. To believe and not to see! I try as hard as I can, but I am not able to solve the rebus." [III, 206]

The panorama from his window merely confuses Georgy Vasilevich. In an attempt to solve the rebus (i.e., to join the individual pictures together and to make sense of the whole), he tries looking at the site through binoculars. The incomprehensible general scene gives way to a series of incomprehensible particular scenes. Georgy Vasilevich picks out people whom the reader recognizes as Ishchenko, Fenya, Saenko, Zagirov, and Seroshevsky; but who they are, and what relation they bear to the building of Magnitogorsk remains a mystery to the confused writer.

Significantly, Georgy Vasilevich turns from the incomprehensible scene with the phrase "creeping empiricism" on his lips. Without a moral or ideological viewpoint he cannot cope with the empiricism of his task. There is too much to describe. Where is he to begin? Only when Vinkich and Triger tell him what each separate person and object has to do with the overall aim, and encourage him to become personally involved, does he begin to understand: "Things and people took on a perceptible interrelationship. They stopped being nameless and dumb. Vinkich liberally endowed them with names and characteristics" (III, 257). From Triger he learns that the entire scope of Soviet industrialization is beyond any one man's power to depict, but there is no need to attempt such a view, for a more limited one will have the same result, just as a raindrop can reflect a whole garden. Thus, with the help of the journalists Georgy Vasilevich begins to understand what is happening at Magnitogorsk, and eventually he lends a practical hand, whereas without a personal commitment he would have continued to be disoriented by the "creeping empiricism" of what he saw.

It is interesting to compare this entire incident with the section near the end of *The Grass of Oblivion* analyzing the nature and limitations of Bunin's talent. Though more will be said about this in a later chapter, for the moment it is worth noting that Kataev considers that Bunin is technically an unsurpassed master, but that he lacks the "external moral pressure" to deal with the "thousand-headed hydra of empiricism" (IX, 433). The mention of Mayakovsky and Magnitogorsk in this same section of the work indicates that Kataev believes them to have been instrumental in enabling him to deal with "empiricism" as Georgy Vasilevich deals with it, i.e., by becoming personally involved and adopting an ideologically committed stance.

In his report to the Seventeenth Congress of the Soviet Communist Party, Kataev claimed that the style of *Time, Forward!* owed much to that of Stalin: "Incidentally, Stalin's style—precise, clear, unusually rich rhythmically—gave me the basic syntactic form."[15] He then goes on to quote the extract from a speech by Stalin which he had twice incorporated into his novel. While it must be admitted that such deference to Stalin's expertise in linguistic matters was common at this time, there is more substance to Kataev's claim than to most others. Stalin's short phrases with their hypnotically frequent repetition of key words and total avoidance of linking devices such as conjunctions and relative pronouns certainly resemble the majority of Kataev's own sentences in *Time, Forward!* It may, however, be more accurate to speak of coincidence rather than imitation, for Kataev employed a similar style in some earlier works, notably "In Winter."

A very large number of sentences in *Time, Forward!* are simple ones. Relative and participial clauses are few, their function being taken over by repetition in a new sentence: "Time is concentrated. It flies. It constrains. One must tear oneself free from it, jump out of it. It must be outstripped" (III, 188). In many cases the avoidance of subordinate or coordinate clauses results in stark, concentrated sentences consisting of subject plus verb, or even just one of those elements.[16] But even where Kataev makes some use of participles, his sentences remain quite short, and the pronominal subjects recur with surprising regularity: "The strong, white sun burned in the window with the speed of magnesium ribbon. But, having penetrated the corridor, it immediately lost its major allies—the dust and the wind. It lost its wild, steppe fierceness. Made harmless by glass, it spread itself over the entire length of the ocher-colored celluloid floor. It pretended to be tame and good-natured, like a cat" (III, 134).

Normal syntax frequently yields to the listing of objects, and many sentences consist almost exclusively of nouns: "To the East go clouds, elevators, fences, Mordovian sarafans, pumphouses, tracked vehicles, freight trains, churches, minarets" (III, 137). Similar examples could be drawn from almost any chapter of the novel. These long lists generally consist of an incongruous mixture of objects and natural phenomena, combined in an apparently random fashion. In this way Kataev tries to suggest, in the first place, the variety of activity at Magnitogorsk. Second, the listing device is part of the cinematic technique; it is the equivalent of the roving camera, appearing to pick out various objects at random, but in fact composing a picture and creating an atmosphere. Third, by reducing normal syntax to lists, Kataev implies that the mass of impressions crowding in on the writer force him to alter the normal pace of his writing. In an age of rapid change the writer's notebook becomes part of the finished work.[17]

Very little in Magnitogorsk stands still for long. People and machines rush around, and so too does the landscape, which is constantly in motion:[18] "Everything moved from its place. Everything began to walk. The trees walked. The grove was wading across the flooded river" (III, 137). In another example, the landscape viewed from a stationary train changes almost as swiftly as if the train were moving, so fundamentally is nature being altered by man: "Opposite the carriage windows, red mountains of clay rose up, or the craters of foundation-pits yawned, and distant water gleamed; bridges and portable cranes being transported on trolleys flashed by; booths, sheds, posts, barrels appeared and suddenly disappeared and then appeared again like so many stations" (III, 268).

The immense scale of this constantly fluid landscape deceives the eye by rendering huge objects tiny. Time and again Kataev mentions the confusion his characters feel at the size of objects (in this case the object in question is a large grain elevator):

At the foot of the middle [hill], something stood in the steppe. Something like a small cube. They got nearer—and it was no longer a cube, but a zinc box standing on end. Such boxes were used to carry bullets at the front. However, the steppe deceives the eyes greatly. One cannot immediately grasp whether an object which is standing in the steppe is large or small. When they got nearer still this zinc box suddenly covered a quarter of the steppe and half the sky. [III, 168][19]

The long, eclectic lists of objects and the play with proportions form part of a central feature of *Time, Forward!*, namely the attempt to convey the atmosphere of confusion and excitement created by the rapid transformation of an agricultural land into an industrial one. Another device which works along the same lines is the description of the outcome of an action or situation before the situation itself. For example, Chapter 6 opens with a bewildering, surrealistic description of a tortoise, a jaded old horse, and a bicycle; only later does the reader learn that these are painted on posters, and meant to represent the current achievements of the three brigade-leaders. Similarly, Chapter 67 begins with the strange sensations experienced by Bixby, and only later is it explained that he has taken morphine. A simpler example of this form of "making it strange"—to use Shklovsky's well-known phrase—occurs on the first page of the novel, where Kataev gives several mathematical calculations with no explanatory context. Only later does he reveal that Margulies is working out the feasibility of beating the record newly set by workers at Kharkov.

It is tempting to relate the inversion of event and result to the general theme of *Time, Forward!*—the outstripping of the old, nineteenth-century view of time—but it must be remembered that Kataev had used a similar device in *The Embezzlers* and several other stories of the 1920s to convey illness, drunkenness, or great stress. In general, *Time, Forward!* demonstrates Kataev's ability to adapt features of his work to the new conditions of the 1930s, and the style of his novel does not represent a radical change from earlier stories.

Time, Forward! contains a far wider range of intonation than any earlier work by Kataev, if by intonation we mean emotional coloring, conveyed by choice of words and syntax. In the 1920s he had used a variety of intonation, including lyricism ("The Father"), warm humor ("The Child"), and satire (scores of sketches and *The Embezzlers*), but the range of intonation within any one work remained limited throughout the decade. In *Time, Forward!* all of these different intonations may be found. The lyricism and the unusual imagery of "The Father" recur in some of the nature descriptions: "Road of lilies-of-the-valley and of nightingales. The nightingales are not afraid of the train. Their song rings out all night. The sharp, glassy trill gurgles through the clay bottleneck of night. The night is filled to the brim with icy dew" (III, 138). Fenya and, to a lesser extent, Margulies are described with warm humor. In his portrayal of Ray Roope and Nalbandov, Kataev uses a sarcastic intonation similar to that in "The Gold Nib." The American's smugness and love of comfort ooze through his veneer of patronizing interest in Magnitogorsk: "Mr. Ray Roope nodded benevolently, and screwed up his eyes. Clasping his small, plump hands across his stomach he glanced alternately at Seroshevsky and his interpreter. Then, with a slight movement of his head and an arch little laugh he would interrupt Mr. Leonard Darley and ask him to translate something"

(III, 202). Finally, Kataev introduces an elevated, hortatory intonation conveying patriotism and support for the spirit of socialist competition: "May not a single trifle, not even the tiniest detail of our inimitable, heroic days of the first Five Year Plan be forgotten" (III, 428).

In its use of imagery, as in certain aspects of characterization, *Time, Forward!* continues the pattern set in the previous decade: "The air broke softly, like a slate board" (III, 132); "the train came out of the barrel of the tunnel like a ramrod" (III, 139); "the alarm clock jangled like a tin of sweets" (III, 131). As may be seen from the first and third of these examples, Kataev's liking for domestic imagery does not entirely disappear, but the most important recurrent feature of the imagery in *Time, Forward!* is its military nature. The building site resembles a battlefront, grotesquely scarred by the trenches of foundation-pits; the workers are frontline soldiers fighting against time and nature, and using as weapons concrete-mixers with all the attributes of heavy guns. When Ishchenko cries "to your wheelbarrows" at the beginning of the decisive shift, it echoes (and perhaps very slightly parodies) a Civil War commander's "to horse" at the start of a battle.[20]

Several similes in the novel are extended, in the Gogolian manner, to the point where the comparison is forgotten, and the object introduced by the comparison achieves a density of detail that draws attention to it in its own right. For example, upon returning to Moscow from Magnitogorsk, one notices that trees, which are completely absent in the steppe, begin to reappear, at first slowly, and then in greater and greater numbers. Kataev makes this point in the following extended simile:

The trees wandered along, like new recruits lagging behind an army. Then the trees began to walk in a drawn-out chain of platoons and companies. Then, with the songs and whistles of nightingales, appeared regiments and divisions. Armies of shaggy conquerors crossed the mountains. They were returning home, covered with the multicolored glory of the rainbow. [III, 422–23]

Shklovsky has suggested that such images draw attention to themselves instead of serving the novel's overall purpose.[21] But in defense of the extended images it may be argued that, together with the shorter similes, they provide a background of differing textures and colors that contrasts sharply with the monochromatic fore-ground. Without the adventurous imagery, *Time, Forward!* would present too stark a picture; it would operate at too abstract a level, for its main characters are drawn up in opposing lines. It is saved from this abstraction by the wealth of detail in the background.

As the work of a fellow-traveler in the process of "transforming himself" into an active supporter of the regime, *Time, Forward!* marked a very important transitional point in Kataev's career, as he has frequently reminded his readers:

For almost a year and a half I worked with exceptional enthusiasm on my chronicle *Time, Forward!* This period of work was in many respects a turning point for me. Until then I had, as it were, written blindly, relying more on feeling than on reason. Feeling is, of course, absolutely essential for a writer, but if it is not illuminated by reason, not subordinated to an idea—in the full sense of the word—then the result will not be a true work of art. Real beauty in art is a synthesis of feeling and reason.[22]

These words touch on a common theme in discussions of Soviet literature of the 1930s, and they can be applied to all of the fellow-travelers whose work changed direction at this time. But they are particularly appropriate for Kataev because of his awareness of the opposing artistic tendencies within himself that were symbolized years later in *The Grass of Oblivion* by the figures of Bunin and Mayakovsky. The problem of how to reconcile feeling and reason, artistry with the demands of ideology, was the basic one facing fellow-travelers at the beginning of the new era in Soviet literature. The answer that Kataev advances through the figure of Georgy Vasilevich—namely, that ideology provides a point of view from which to approach the vast, incomprehensible material world—remains the cornerstone of his artistic faith (at least as expressed in his formal declarations) to the present day. The artistic success of *Time, Forward!* springs from the fact that "reason" (or ideology) does not swamp "feeling." As Shklovsky was quick to point out, the strength of the novel is Kataev's old strength—imagery and the rendering of atmosphere.[23] Some contemporary critics objected that *Time, Forward!* revealed technological ignorance, or that it offered a stylized rather than a realistic view of socialist construction.[24] There is some truth in these comments, but they appear faintly ridiculous because they make no allowance for the element of "feeling." By adapting the strong points of his earlier work to new conditions, Kataev produced a novel that may err in substance, but that conveys, as few other works do, the spirit and atmosphere of the early years of the period of socialist construction.

II   Lone White Sail

Kataev's second novel of the 1930s was *Lone White Sail*, which first appeared in 1936. It is the story of a significant year in the lives of two eight-year-old boys, Petya Bachey, the son of a schoolmaster, and his friend Gavrik Chernoivanenko, the grandson of a poor fisherman. For both boys, 1905 brings important changes in their personal lives—Petya begins to attend school, and Gavrik's grandfather dies—and on a wider scale Russia is shaken by revolution. In Odessa the crew of the battleship *Potemkin* mutiny and take the ship to Rumania. One member of the crew, Rodion Zhukov, returns to Odessa and, after a narrow escape from the police, is saved from drowning by Gavrik and his grandfather. Gradually the two boys are drawn into the revolutionary struggle through their relationship with Zhukov and Gavrik's elder brother, who is also a Bolshevik. When armed insurrection breaks out, Gavrik and Petya carry ammunition past the police lines to the rebels. Gavrik knows what he is doing, but Petya merely carries out the orders of his friend, whose "slave" he has become as the result of losing heavily at a gambling game. The revolution finally comes to nothing, but the boys help Zhukov to escape from Odessa so that he can carry on his work elsewhere.

The boys' small part in the 1905 revolution forms the principal element in the plot, but equally important are the many set scenes which evoke the atmosphere of Odessa in the early years of the century: Petya's journey on board an ancient steamship; Gavrik's excitement on visiting the fairground; Petya's school entrance examination; a young boy's sense of wonder at the sight of a Christmas tree.

Lone White Sail bears such a striking resemblance to Mark Twain's novels about childhood, particularly *The Adventures of Tom Sawyer*, that one is forced to the conclusion that the American author must have influenced Kataev, even if only subconsciously. Both *Lone White Sail* and *Tom Sawyer* are imbued with a warm, lyrical, humorous nostalgia for childhood. The relationship between the central characters of both books is almost identical: a motherless schoolboy is befriended by a waif, and the schoolboy's conventional education is greatly enriched by the friendship; he comes into contact with a world very different from the secure one of his home. Both novels are full of childhood lore, the hundreds of beliefs, superstitions, and turns of phrase peculiar to the young. There are, of course, many differences between the novels, but there seems little doubt that Kataev drew upon Twain.[25]

Some of the events of *Lone White Sail* correspond broadly to Kataev's own childhood experiences and those of his friends, as he once admitted in an interview: "The boy, Gavrik, for example, really existed. So did his grandfather. They had a small boat in which they went out to sea. I knew Gavrik well and was friendly with him. His real name was Misha Galy. I even have a photograph of him. . . . We did not carry bullets to the insurgents, but they were carried by other boys, friends of ours. So it could have been us" (VIII, 411, 415). In writing about a period which he recalled from his own childhood, with characters based in part on his family and friends, Kataev turned to earlier semiautobiographical works and incorporated them, or drew upon them for his novel. The incident involving Rodion Zhukov, for instance, had already been told in the story of the same name, but in reworking it for inclusion within *Lone White Sail* the author removed the elements of pessimism and fatalism with which he had endowed Zhukov and replaced them by strength, courage, and optimism—more acceptable qualities in the hero of a novel written in the 1930s.

"Ushki" ("Buttons"), a story of 1930, is incorporated into *Lone White Sail* in its entirety, with only a few minor alterations. It tells of the passion for gambling with decorative metal buttons which seized the boys of Odessa in 1905, and of how one of them, Petya Sinaysky, paid his debt to "the street arab" Gavrik by helping him carry "buttons"—which turned out to be bullets—through the police lines to the rebels. The story of the buttons occupies an important place in the novel and survives its transposition very well, largely because of the episodic structure of *Lone White Sail*.

A less obvious, but no less important, antecedent is "More" ("The Sea"), a story dating from 1928. It is essentially a tone poem in which Kataev strives to convey the minute differences in the color and texture of the sea at different times of the day. He concentrates on visual impressions, but does not ignore the other senses, especially smell. No other work demonstrates in such a pure form Kataev's obsession with recording sensuous detail as accurately as possible. Here he emulates the Bunin whom he himself had depicted in "Music" as a relentless seeker after accuracy of description.

Lone White Sail brings together the lyricism of "The Sea," an adventure story based in part on "Rodion Zhukov," and the insight into the psychology and language of children of "Buttons" in a work with much of the spirit of *The Adventures of Tom Sawyer*.

The straightforward construction of the novel rests on the intersection of two story lines—one essentially private, dealing with the everyday life of Petya Bachey and his family and friends, the other public, namely, the story of the 1905 revolution in Odessa and the part played in it by Rodion Zhukov and the two boys. Kataev thus sets a pattern for the other works in his tetralogy. In all four novels (*Lone White Sail, The Small Farm in the Steppe, Winter Wind*, and *The Catacombs*) the opening chapters deal in leisurely fashion with the private preoccupations of Petya Bachey, particularly his reaction to the physical world around him. At this early stage of all four works the rumbling threats of social upheaval remain in the background. Then, toward the middle of each book the enclosed world of the hero's private concerns opens out, and his life is viewed in the context of historical events. This change of focus entails a change in style from predominantly descriptive and digressive to predominantly narrative. In the binary construction of each novel of the tetralogy can be seen a reflection of the split in Kataev's creative personality between the aesthete, responsible for the early chapters in which the hero's sensuous awareness of the world is convincingly recorded, and the committed Soviet writer, responsible for the pro-revolutionary narrative.

The adult characters of *Lone White Sail* are drawn with very little subtlety or complexity. Rodion Zhukov and Terenty Chernoivanenko, Gavrik's grandfather, and even Petya's father play conventional, indeed stereotyped roles in the plot. Only at rare moments does Kataev go beyond the requirements of the narrative to give these characters individual features, as in the humorous and touching scene where Gavrik's grandfather speaks to his miracle-working icon.

In contrast to the flat, uninspired characterization of the adults in *Lone White Sail*, the children are drawn with convincing authority. Whereas Kataev views the adult characters purely from the outside, in the case of the children he recalls vividly from his own experience the excitement of young people who are gradually getting to know the world and for whom its many sights, sounds, and smells have not yet become so familiar as to pass unnoticed.

A recurring feature of the characterization of children in the novel is the use of semidirect speech, by means of which Kataev may change the point of view freely from that of an adult to that of a child, as in the following example:

Little Pavlik, dressed for the journey in a new blue smock and a stiffly starched pique hat shaped like a jelly-mold, stood at a prudent distance from the horses and pondered every detail of their harnesses. He was quite astonished by the fact that these harnesses—real harnesses on real live horses—were obviously constructed differently from the one on his beautiful cardboard horse Kudlatka. (They hadn't bought Kudlatka on vacation with them and he was now awaiting his master's return in Odessa.) Probably the shop assistant who had sold Kudlatka had got things mixed up somehow. Anyway, he would have to remember to ask Daddy as soon as they got back to cut something up and make some of those lovely black patch things—whatever they were called—and sew them on to Kudlatka's eyes. [V, 18]

The point of view in the early part of this extract is that of the author, who observes and describes Pavlik (Petya's three-year-old brother). In the later part he begins to record Pavlik's thought, without any formal indication through quotation marks of a change in the point of view. This device allows the author to create the illusion that he is in a state of sympathetic complicity with his young character, and yet at the same time superior to him and able to mock gently his limitations.

From his very early stories onwards Kataev had approached his semiautobiographical heroes with a mixture of affection and deflating irony. His attitude to Petya Bachey in *Lone White Sail* is in the same tradition. Petya is dreamy, introspective, excessively sensitive and proud, and greatly influenced by reading. His personality emerges clearly in Chapter 2, where, while others prepare for departure, he enjoys a solitary and self-indulgently melancholy stroll and swim, accompanied in imagination by the heroes of his favorite books, such as Robinson Crusoe. More powerful even than the image of Crusoe, however, is the effect on Petya's imagination of Mikhail Lermontov's poem "The Sail," the first line of which serves as the novel's title. The great Romantic poet's lines about a lone white sail, proud and rebellious on the blue sea, strike a responsive chord in Petya's soul, and in his mind he plays the role of the solitary, proud rebel. When he sees the *Potemkin* steaming off the coast of Bessarabia, it seems to him to be a kindred spirit, and the words he chooses to describe it come from Lermontov's poem.

Petya's image of himself as a solitary Romantic hero does not go unchallenged by Kataev. At the school entrance examination he chooses to recite "The Sail," but the examiners interrupt his performance before the crucial final stanza—a gently ironic comment on the character's conceit.

Like some other characters of Kataev's, Petya has a passion for gambling which drives him to extraordinary lengths. When the urge to gamble with buttons takes hold of him, it dominates his personality, causing him to steal, lie, and make false accusations, and yet this apparently destructive passion brings a sweet intensity to his life which is irresistible. Petya's gambling represents a further application of the author's favorite device of the 1920s—the abnormal state of mind that causes a character to undergo a radical, if temporary, change.

As in the case of *Time, Forward!*, the real strength of *Lone White Sail* lies not in plot or characterization, but in the evocation of a particular period that the author had lived through.[26] By attention to detail Kataev conveys the atmosphere of Odessa in 1905 as it appeared to a sensitive boy. Among other ways, the novel captures the atmosphere of pre-revolutionary Odessa through the use of brand names and street names. Gavrik shoots with a "Montecristo" rifle and drinks "Fialka" lemonade; Pavlik eats "George Borman" boiled sweets; the policeman who arrests grandfather smokes an "Asmolov" cigarette. Odessa's colorful markets and fairgrounds, its kvass-sellers, organ-grinders, and chambermaids all form part of the densely textured background to the adventure story. Many of the descriptions do not advance the narrative but form self-contained digressions which contribute much to the novel's atmosphere.

As important for the atmosphere as these period details of everyday life in Odessa is the vast amount of childhood lore in *Lone White Sail*. The reader learns, for example, that the children of Odessa believed that organ-grinders were abductors who sold children to fairgrounds; that a certain brand of sweets were held to be poisonous; that ice cream was thought to be made from milk in which invalids had bathed. *Lone White Sail* is full of such details, and the interaction between the engaging, if superficial, narrative on the one hand and the detailed picture of an Odessa childhood on the other lends the book its specific charm.

Socialist Realism requires that works should be accessible to unsophisticated readers, and that therefore style should be simplified and unusual imagery of the sort that had been common in the 1920s removed. In an article of 1933 Kataev had expressed the wish to write more simply, in particular to reduce the number of metaphors in his work.[27] Seeking, as usual in these years, to adapt his writing to current demands, Kataev was determined to simplify his style. But the style of *Lone White Sail* does not represent a radical departure from much of his earlier work. The lyricism, the concrete descriptions of physical objects, the sensuous evocation of a scene— all of these features find their way into the novel. Only in the more restrained use of unusual metaphors and similes does the style reflect an effort at simplification. Such images as remain utilize familiar objects, and draw attention to purely superficial similarities in shape or texture: fine sand is said to resemble semolina; a jellyfish in the water is like a transparent lampshade; a fine spray hangs in the air like a sheet of muslin. These typical images are somewhat bland, lacking the exciting, exotic quality of those in the best of Kataev's earlier work.

The outstanding feature of the descriptive passages in *Lone White Sail* is undoubtedly their sensuousness. Kataev recreates in words the sharp smell of wildflowers, the sights, sounds, and smells of the fishmarket or the fair, the taste of lemonade, the painful coldness of well water, the feel of sand under the feet. Sometimes an experience is conveyed by means of its effect on several or all of the senses, as in the scene where Gavrik fires a rifle at the fairgound and tastes the residue of the gunpowder as it hangs in the air in addition to smelling it and hearing the crack of the shot. In passages like this, despite the vast and growing differences between them, one can still see the affinity between Kataev and Bunin, for whom such moments and their recreation in art were of great importance.

III   I, a Son of the Working People

After completing *Lone White Sail*, Kataev intended to write further works based on the lives of Petya Bachey and Gavrik Chernoivanenko. He orignally appears to have envisaged a cycle of six novels,[28] but, as he later put it, "world events occurred which interfered with my plans" (VIII, 410). Instead of the projected novel about the adolescence of Petya and Gavrik, to which he returned only in 1956, Kataev produced in 1937 *I, a Son of the Working People*, a tale set in the Ukraine during the German occupation of 1918, and the weakest of the longer works of this period.

Twice before in the 1930s Kataev had turned to the epoch of the Civil War, and each time he had viewed the period through a prism of nostalgia as a distant, romantic age, a "uniquely wonderful time" (I, 429). In "Chernyi khleb" ("Black Bread," 1935) he recalls his days as a journalist in Kharkov in 1921 when he had frequently gone hungry but had been enchanted by the excitement and idealism of the age. "Son" ("Sleep," 1933) is a modern folk tale about the Red Army commander Semyon Budenny who, like the hero of a medieval Russian epic tale, stands guard while his exhausted army sleeps. In *I, a Son of the Working People*, the Civil War seems equally distant—a romantic period of history as far removed from life in the 1930s as the medieval setting of Gogol's *Taras Bulba*, which clearly influenced the work.

The hero of *I, a Son of the Working People*, a peasant named Semyon Kotko, fights in World War I, but when the Civil War breaks out he chooses not to join the Red Army, preferring to return to his farm and his fiancée. Despite her father's objections to the match, preparations for the wedding go ahead, but before it can take place the Germans occupy the village and hang two Bolshevik leaders. Semyon is forced to flee to the Red Army. On hearing that his fiancée is to be forced to marry the reinstated landowner, Semyon returns to the village in time to stop the wedding but is captured and sentenced to death. Saved by the intervention of the Bolsheviks, he realizes the folly of his wish to live in peace before the Civil War is won. Finally, in an epilogue set in the 1930s Semyon and his wife watch proudly as their son, along with thousands of other young soldiers, takes his oath of allegiance (from which the work's title is drawn).

The most remarkable feature of the tale is the way in which Kataev attempts to transform his inability to portray individual adult characters into a virtue by making his central figure a folk hero. As one reviewer remarked: "Semyon expresses himself like the collective hero of a folk tale. His speech is full of the beauty of legend, but, of course, his are not the concrete words of a particular hero."[29] By 1937 the doctrine of Socialist Realism had provided theoretical justification for the use of "typical" rather than particular heroes, and Kataev's work was welcomed by one establishment critic as a step forward.[30] The opening sentence ("A soldier was returning from the front") indicates the author's wish to make his hero a universal figure whose experiences were those of the mass of the people in the Civil War. However, his use of folk motifs and language militates against this intention by so distancing the story that it appears quaint rather than moving. Such is the degree of stylization introduced by the folk language that any semblance of realism in the portrayal of historical events is destroyed. In spite of an attempt to relate past and present through the epilogue, the Civil War as depicted in this work is no less remote than the exploits of Prince Igor in *The Lay of Igor's Campaign.*

One major influence on *I, a Son of the Working People* is, then, folk literature. Another is the work of Gogol, especially *Evenings on a Farm near Dikanka* and *Taras Bulba.* The latter work deals with a broadly similar theme, and several passages in Kataev's tale can be shown to have been directly inspired by it,[31] but the descriptions of everyday Ukrainian life in *Evenings on a Farm near Dikanka* are much closer to Kataev's natural mode, and Gogol's early work has left a deeper imprint on *I, a Son of the Working People* than the superficially more similar *Taras Bulba.* The best chapters of Kataev's tale, describing the ritual surrounding a Ukrainian betrothal, capture some of the Gogolian spirit. It is worth noting that only in these chapters does Kataev subordinate action to description. These leisurely, digressive chapters, full of specific references to local customs, show that Kataev was still the sharp observer of everyday life whom Mashbits-Verov and others had criticized, but he now carefully incorporated his chronicling of everyday life within an ideologically unimpeachable narrative.

In each of his longer works of the 1930s Kataev succeeds in combining certain of his established strengths with a degree of active support for the regime; this made his work politically acceptable in the age of Socialist Realism. From the publication of *Time, Forward!* onward Kataev's position as a *Soviet* author (in the sense of an orthodox writer working within the framework of Socialist Realism) was rarely questioned. Yet all of his works of the 1930s reveal in patches those qualities that had made him a lively and talented fellow-traveler during the 1920s. The humor, the interest in every-day details, the lyricism, and even the depiction of delirium and other deranging conditions are all present to some degree, albeit greatly diluted. Even that sensuousness and aestheticism that linked Kataev to his mentor Bunin does not disappear entirely in the works of Socialist Realism, although it is heavily overlaid by adventure plots and the expression of somewhat simplistic pro-revolutionary sentiments.

CHAPTER 5

Marking Time

I N terms of the quality of his works, the years from the entry of the Soviet Union into World War II to the beginning of the 1960s were the bleakest in Kataev's career, a period when he returned time and time again to ground which he had already covered more successfully in the 1930s. For twenty years he marked time, and it is tempting to interpret the anguished cry of his autobiographical narrator in *The Holy Well* ("Who will return wasted time to me?", IX, 180) as a reference to this creative lull. The suspicions of one critic that Kataev's middle period was his worst turned out to be well founded.[1]

I War Stories

The best of Kataev's short stories about World War II achieve their effect through sharp incongruity. Some are purely anecdotal, others more substantial, but almost without exception they are constructed around a touching, sentimental, or horrific contrast. In "Kontsert pered boem" ("A Concert before the Battle," 1942) a famous singer of Russian folk songs tells of singing to soldiers on the eve of battle and of performing for dying men in a field hospital.[2] "Leitenant" ("The Lieutenant," 1942) exploits the contrast between a humdrum Party meeting and the context in which it occurs: a desperate struggle for military survival. The lieutenant of the title has to leave the meeting just as his application for Party membership is about to be discussed because an alarm warns of an enemy air attack. In the ensuing battle he is mortally wounded, but manages to land his fighter plane safely. The meeting continues, and the lieutenant is posthumously elected to Party membership.[3] In "Flag" ("The Flag," 1942) a small Soviet garrison on a beleaguered island refuses to comply with a German order to fly a white flag. Instead the men sew together a huge red flag and hoist it during the night.

At dawn, the confident German commander sees what he takes to be a white flag, assuming that its color can be explained by the rising sun; but as the sun rises higher the flag remains red, and the commander issues the order to destroy the island. Here the heroism of the island's defenders is distilled into a poetic—one might almost say an operatic—detail, typical of Kataev's approach to this theme. (Another example occurs in the novel *For the Power of the Soviets*, where the heroine goes to her execution with a white acacia twig between her teeth.) In perhaps the best of his war stories, "Viaduk" ("The Viaduct," 1946), Kataev abandons the highly dramatic use of contrast and incongruous detail in favor of a bald narrative style and unsentimental understatement, which makes the death of one of the central characters very moving. However, although contrast is not dramatic in this story, it does exist: as usual, Kataev places the military incident within a framework of everyday, peaceful activities. "Otche nash" ("Our Father," 1946) reveals Kataev's sympathy with the plight of children caught up in war, a subject which preoccupied him for much of the 1940s. Fearing deportation and death, a Jewish mother and her young son leave their home in occupied Odessa one winter day and walk the city streets until they drop, exhausted, onto a park bench and freeze to death. The pathos of their sorry fate is heightened by the fact that each morning the Lord's Prayer is read in Rumanian by a child and broadcast over loudspeakers in the streets. There is a shocking incongruity between the wooden sound of the Jewish boy's frozen body bouncing off the floor of the truck into which it is thrown and the simultaneous tender sound of a child's voice reciting the Lord's Prayer.

The long story *Zhena* (*The Wife*, 1943) is dedicated to the memory of Kataev's brother, Evgeny Petrov.[4] On the surface, this work appears to have nothing to do with Petrov's death, but on closer examination it becomes clear that Kataev's bereavement accounts for much in the tale that puzzled contemporary critics. It is the story of an encounter between a war correspondent and a young woman who has come to the front to find her husband's grave. While they wait for a Soviet attack to be mounted she tells him the story of her courtship and marriage, of her work in a munitions factory, and of the death of her husband.

One reviewer of *The Wife* criticized Kataev for being more interested in describing the peaceful scenes in prewar Sebastopol and the brief period that the young couple spent at the Hotel Moskva in Moscow before the husband returned to his unit than in dealing with the war and the work of the munitions factory.[5] The reviewer was correct in that assessment, for the best pages are indeed devoted to the first meeting of the young couple in the Crimea. So blissful is Nina's holiday in Sebastopol, and so full of the promise of happiness is her brief marriage to Andrey, that the intrusion of war comes as a great shock. It is as if Kataev shares his heroine's grief, as if he too prefers to recall the South in summer and the Hotel Moskva, where he had last seen his brother alive, rather than turn to the problems of the present. Kataev's personal bereavement adds poignancy to his nostalgic descriptions of a peaceful and stable prewar life and of brief meetings between Nina and Andrey in the Hotel Moskva during the war. Compared with this warm and touching (if sentimental) wave of nostalgia, the description of socialist competition in the munitions factory appears quite mechanical, nothing more than a dry repetition of certain aspects of *Time, Forward!* What distinguishes *The Wife* and mitigates its sentimentality is its oblique tribute to the memory of Evgeny Petrov.

Kataev's two remaining longer tales of the 1940s both return to the subject of children. Of *Elektricheskaia mashina (The Electric Machine,* 1943) little need be said, for it acts as a pendant to *Lone White Sail,* and its distinguishing features are those of the earlier novel. Once again Kataev explores the relationship between Petya and Gavrik, but this time in a situation where the former plays the dominating role. Petya's infectious wish to make "an electric machine" leads Gavrik to waste some hard-earned money. The characterization, the dialogue, and the concrete descriptions are all excellent and lend this story a charm that the more celebrated *Syn polka (Son of the Regiment)* lacks. It may well be significant that in the year in which he produced the nostalgic tale *The Wife* Kataev should also have written a story that looks back to his childhood and recaptures the atmosphere of *Lone White Sail.* Petrov's death undoubtedly accounts for much in *The Wife;* it may also explain why *The Electric Machine*—Kataev's only work of the period that does not deal in some way with the war—should have been written in 1943, at the height of hostilities.

Son of the Regiment, first published in 1945, gained a Stalin prize for Kataev, but its success (it is still frequently republished) hardly seems merited. It may excel by comparison with other books about orphaned children in the war, of which there were several, but that is more a reflection of the poor quality of the other works than a sign of any great merit in Kataev's. This tale of an orphaned boy who is "adopted" by a regiment, and who helps the soldiers in reconnaissance work, has little of the delightful, evocative atmosphere of *Lone White Sail* and *The Electric Machine*. Whereas Kataev knew what it felt like to be Petya Bachey, he remains outside Vanya Solntsev, the "son of the regiment." Petya is an individual boy with a specific view of the world around him, whereas Vanya is representative. In this contrast one sees as clearly as anywhere in Kataev's work the author's preference for autobiographical characters over imagined ones, even in the case of children.

II   For the Power of the Soviets

Kataev's visits to Odessa immediately after its liberation gave him the idea of writing a sequel to *Lone White Sail* in which Petya and Gavrik would appear as partisans. His first attempt at the theme— a non-fictional account of the underground resistance entitled "The Catacombs"—presents a romantic picture of the partisans, dwelling on the excitement and comradeship of life in the catacombs rather than its physical difficulties.[6] The partisans of "The Catacombs" served as prototypes for the central figures in Kataev's novel, and herein lies the major difficulty facing the author. On the one hand, the central characters in *For the Power of the Soviets* are brave, resourceful members of the resistance; on the other hand, they are adult versions of the heroes of *Lone White Sail*. This duality deals the novel a severe blow. Kataev seems uncertain whether to write a modern war novel or to try to recapture the atmosphere of his earlier work, whether to write for an adult readership or for children.[7]

The central figures in *For the Power of the Soviets* are the Moscow lawyer, Petr Vasilevich Bachey (the former Petya Bachey), and the Odessa Party Secretary, Gavrik Chernoivanenko. Petr Vasilevich and his young son Petya are on holiday in Odessa when war breaks out. Petr Vasilevich joins the army and little Petya enters the catacombs to join Gavrik's partisans. After many adventures father and son are eventually reunited in the catacombs, and the band emerges at the end of the war after waging a constant secret battle against the German and Rumanian occupation forces.

At first greeted with positive reviews, the novel was then subjected to a long and highly critical appraisal in *Pravda* in 1950 by the staunchly orthodox critic and author of Socialist Realist novels, Mikhail Bubennov.[8] Bubennov's criticism reveals much both about Kataev's novel and about the attitudes prevailing in the Zhdanov period.

Bubennov's first stricture concerns the appearance, manner of speech, and character of the local Party Secretary, Gavrik Chernoivanenko. He objects to the use of the childhood nickname Gavrik, and argues that Chernoivanenko is an unsuitable person for the post of Party Secretary by virtue of his cold, unfeeling personality, his lack of organizational ability (he goes into the catacombs with inadequate equipment), and his attitude toward life in the catacombs, which is based on romantic adventure tales rather than on a realistic appraisal of the situation. Second, Bubennov objects to the implication that Chernoivanenko's group of partisans was left to fend for itself, unaided by the central Party organization. Third, he contends that Kataev devotes too much space to depicting the everyday lives of the partisans, (what is known in Russian as *byt*), and too little space to their military activities. A related point is what he terms Kataev's over-reliance on coincidence and on the recollection of his heroes' childhood. As he puts it: "In his quest for an entertaining plot V. Kataev often descends to the level of the detective novel." Finally, Bubennov criticizes the novel's language, which he finds too colloquial in places. He ends his review by rebuking the editors of *Novy mir* for publishing the work, and expresses the desire that it be carefully rewritten.

A few days after the publication of this review a letter signed by Kataev appeared in *Pravda* in which the author admitted that the criticism of his novel was "just and principled" and promised to revise the work radically.[9] After a further eighteen months' work on *For the Power of the Soviets*, a second version appeared in 1951. However, this version failed to satisfy Kataev, and in 1961 he revised it again for inclusion in his tetralogy, this time changing the title to *The Catacombs*.

Most of the changes in the novel fit one or another of the categories suggested by Bubennov. The first of these is the character of the Party Secretary. In the first version of the novel the Party Secretary is referred to throughout as Gavrik, no doubt because Kataev had before him the image of the young hero of *Lone White Sail*. Following the critic's suggestion, Kataev changed this to the

more formal Gavriil Semyonovich in the second version and retained
this name in the third version, allowing his hero to be called Gavrik
only by his childhood friends. The Gavrik of the first version has
an unpleasant face, an irritating, high-pitched voice, and he frequently uses Odessa jargon. Moreover, he gives the impression of
being rootless, almost Bohemian. A bachelor, he lives in an untidy
flat and appears to lack recreational interests. In the late 1940s such
an image of a Party Secretary could not pass uncensured. The hero
of the second version conforms more closely to the current ster-
eotype of Party Secretary.[10] He no longer has a squeaky voice, and
his language has been purged of local slang. He is now a widower
who remains faithful to the memory of his wife and lives in a neat
little home with flowers on the windowsill. Most important of all,
he no longer idles away his time in recollections of childhood, but
works efficiently as a Party official, and even devotes himself to
historical research. In the third version Kataev retained most of
these changes, reintroducing only some of the character's colorful
speech from the original version.

The second major area of change concerns Party control over the
partisans, the subject of Bubennov's most serious criticism. In the
first version, Gavrik alone decides to set up a resistance group and
enter the catacombs. There is no reason to believe that anyone in
Moscow, least of all Stalin, knows of the group's existence. This
state of affairs changes in the second version, in which the charge
of insularity is answered by the inclusion of a new episode involving
a Party official who parachutes into Odessa to transmit Party orders
to the resistance workers. His immediate superior is "Nikita Ser-
geevich" (Khrushchev), but he implies that Stalin himself has probably heard of the exploits of the Odessa partisans. Stalin even
appears in person in two new scenes in the second version. Kataev
clearly wished to avoid further criticism of spontaneous individu-
alism on the part of his characters! The third version steers a middle
course, retaining the episode with the central Party official, but
omitting all references to political leaders, including Khrushchev.

The third type of change introduced into the novel additional
scenes of action against the Germans. Kataev has said explicitly that
such scenes as the blowing up of the harbor were forced upon him
against his better judgment, and he has omitted them from the
definitive third version.[11] Some of these episodes are well told, but
they remain self-contained stories grafted onto a novel.

An important area of change involves reminiscence. At least in retrospect, Kataev was well aware of the danger of following *Lone White Sail* with a sequel set almost forty years later.[12] The problem is that the heroes frequently reminisce about one very short period of their lives—the period covered in the earlier novel. The result can, at times, be absurd. The Party Secretary recalls hitting the Moscow lawyer in the eye when both were boys of eight; Petr Vasilevich recalls playing truant to go fishing with Kolesnichuk; even little Petya, born in the 1930s, recalls his father's stories of the Odessa of 1905. Through his overuse of reminiscence Kataev appears to regret that his novel is set in the 1940s rather than in the period of his own childhood. In the succeeding versions the role of reminiscence is greatly reduced, although the third version, written after the other novels in the tetralogy, contains recollections of other periods of the characters' lives.

Even in its definitive version, *For the Power of the Soviets* remains largely an artistic failure. The characters lack complexity, and even the children and young people have no spark of genuine inspiration behind them. Time and again Kataev seeks to compensate for a lack of knowledge of the lives of partisans by delving into his own past. And, as with *Son of the Regiment*, he views his young heroes from the outside rather than from within.

The novel's setting suffers from a similar fault: the author seems less interested in depicting Odessa of the 1940s than Odessa in the early years of the century, when he had lived there. When Petr Vasilevich returns to Odessa after the defeat of his battery, he recalls the money-changers who had once traded on the spot where he is now standing. There is little attempt to describe the features of the modern town, but there is a detailed description of various foreign currencies, and the mysterious way in which they became more or less valuable from minute to minute (VI, 509–10).

For the Power of the Soviets contains a number of lyrical nature descriptions and poetic details that contrast strikingly with the violent narrative. The twig of white acacia held by Valentina on her way to execution has already been mentioned. Other examples include a snowflake which falls into the catacombs via a well, emphasizing the privations of life underground; and the lyrical chapter in which Petr Vasilevich recalls a night he spent on the seashore with a girl in his youth. In this latter example Kataev attributes to the character a poem that he himself had written in 1918, entitled

"Ogni Kassiopei" ("The Fires of Cassiopeia"). The peaceful beauty
of the starry night contrasts with the activity of one of Petr Vasilevich's companions, who is trying to call Moscow on the radio.
Thus, the beauty of nature, poetry, and youthful love intensifies the
ugliness of invasion and occupation by enemy forces. A similar effect
is achieved by the emotional and lyrical description of Moscow in
Chapter 2, and by the sudden change of mood between the end of
Chapter 4, describing little Petya's summer holiday, and the beginning of Chapter 5, in which the invasion begins. As in *The Wife*,
Kataev's approach to the theme of war consists in emphasizing its
disruption of the stability and happiness of peacetime.

Whereas during and immediately after the Civil War Kataev had
written stories about young men for whom life was a joyous experience irrespective of that great social upheaval—whose private life
remained essentially separate from war and politics—he now presents war as an unbearable intrusion which must be ended as soon
as possible if life is to be happy again. During the Civil War Kataev's
heroes contained the seeds of happiness within themselves, in their
youth, good health, love, and poetry; but now happiness depends
on social stability and peace. To some extent, this change in attitude
may be explained by advancing years, for the philosophy of the
Civil War stories is that of a young man. But, more than that, the
change reflects Kataev's increasingly evident view of the relationship between the private and public spheres of life. In such works
as *I, a Son of the Working People* and *The Wife* he had attempted
to show that private happiness cannot be secure without national
security. *For the Power of the Soviets* incorporates the same as-
sumption.

For the Power of the Soviets is an ambitious work, and its failure
illuminates Kataev's strengths and weaknesses as a novelist. Only
when working in the miniature form of individual self-contained
episodes does he reveal his descriptive gifts. At this time the side
of his talent that leaned toward Bunin—his aestheticism—was subordinated to the need for ideological and patriotic orthodoxy. During
the next two decades the aesthete in Kataev would emerge into the
open, slowly and cautiously at first, and then more and more obviously.

III   The Small Farm in the Steppe

Throughout the 1950s Kataev continued to work on the tetralogy
Black Sea Waves, publishing the remaining two volumes in 1956

(The Small Farm in the Steppe) and 1961 *(Winter Wind)*. He thus eventually returned to the work that he had intended to write in 1937, but had postponed for many years in order to write about war.

The Small Farm in the Steppe is set in the years 1910–12, beginning with the death of Tolstoy and ending with the massacre at the Lena goldfields. As in *Lone White Sail*, Kataev attempts to interweave the themes of the growth of revolutionary awareness in the nation and the personal and political development of Petya Bachey. However, the parallel public and private strands remain unintegrated, and the construction is much more labored than in the earlier novel. The work divides into two sections. The first, which could be termed "private," deals with the death of Tolstoy, the sacking of Petya's father, his employment by a private school, and a long description (twenty chapters) of a trip to Europe undertaken by Bachey and his sons; and the second, or "public," section with the revolutionary activities of Zhukov, Terenty, and Gavrik, and the way in which the Bacheys become drawn into them. Kataev uses two very different sources for his novel: his own memories of childhood and his early poems on the one hand,[13] and historical accounts and documents on the other.

The best chapters in the novel display the qualities of the short story, and stand out from the rest of the work. For example, Chapter 7 forms a self-contained digression on the early days of the cinema in Odessa and anticipates *A Mosaic of Life*, which consists entirely of such pieces. Similarly, Chapter 9 is a short story about the obsession that forces Petya and Gavrik to eat a whole jar of strawberry jam. The construction thus suffers from the clash between a series of incidents from domestic life, each of which is complete in itself, and a historical narrative that seeks to place the lives of the heroes in a broader context. A form of construction that had been quite suitable for *Lone White Sail* is here creakingly ponderous.

In other respects, too, *The Small Farm in the Steppe* falls short of its predecessor. Its success lies solely in isolated passages—nature descriptions which make use of Kataev's early poems, flashes of insight into the psychology of adolescents in love, the amused irony with which the author portrays Petya's excessive self-esteem. But the characterization of Petya and his father, which displays several nice touches, loses its subtlety when Kataev insists on their political education. And the portrait of Gavrik retains very little of the charm that it had in *Lone White Sail*.

The Small Farm in the Steppe intermittently reveals the gifts that Kataev had shown in the earlier novel, but it lacks that work's coherence and atmosphere. Its political message is crude and un-integrated, and it relies too heavily on earlier inspiration. But once again it illustrates Kataev's attempt to bring together two very different elements, and in this lies its principal significance for his work. The poetry which he had written under Bunin's direct influence in the second decade of the century is here reworked and incorporated into a novel which also contains the political message he has advanced since the 1930s. Striving to reconcile these two aspects of his work, Kataev produces a novel in which the seams show all too clearly.

IV   Winter Wind

In *Winter Wind* we meet Petya Bachey at a decisive moment in his life, the point when he must take sides in the Civil War. His choice is predictable enough, but his vacillations are depicted with such sympathy that this novel stands out among the work of Kataev's middle period for its complex and interesting central adult character.

After being slightly wounded during the summer offensive of 1917, Petya Bachey is sent to Odessa to recuperate. There he flirts with the many girls who visit him in the hospital, but he soon becomes involved in a more serious affair with Irina, the daughter of General Zarya-Zaryanitsky. Engrossed in his love affair, Petya takes no part in the Revolution, but his old friends Gavrik and Marina—now married to each other—play an important role in the Bolshevik victory. Petya eventually joins the Red Army, forgetting for a while his passion for Irina. During a counter-revolution led by Irina's father, Marina and Petya's brother Pavlik are killed. At their final meeting in wintry Odessa Petya and Irina realize that they have become enemies, and she unsuccessfully attempts to shoot him. The novel ends with an echo of *Lone White Sail*: as the invading German armies occupy the city, the Bolsheviks—including Terenty, Rodion Zhukov, Gavrik, and now Petya—flee in a small boat in order to continue the struggle from afar.

The construction of this work follows a familiar pattern, but this time the integration of personal and historical story-lines is achieved more plausibly than in *The Small Farm in the Steppe*. The first nineteen chapters, in which Petya's private affairs dominate, have an intimacy and freshness of vision lacking in the broader sweep of the later chapters. But the contrast between the two sections does not mar the novel as it had its predecessor, because the construction can be justified by its theme, namely the need to choose between serving the Revolution and following purely private pursuits.

Like Semyon Kotko, Petya Bachey returns home from World War I wishing to enjoy life's pleasures and unwilling to risk his life again. Cocooned from reality by the comfort and safety of the military hospital, he avoids the necessity of an ideological choice. When Marina asks him which side he is on, "it was very difficult to reply. Perhaps even impossible" (VI, 159). Petya's aunt tells him that he cannot remain neutral in the present struggle, he cannot "just live": "My dear, everyone wants to live. But how? How do you want to live? Perhaps the fate of Russia depends on how you intend to live in the future" (VI, 74).

Petya's desire to postpone any choice between sides while leading a life of pleasure is shown to be a temporary condition, a reaction to the years of war from which he eventually emerges. But it is precisely this openness to the variety of life's pleasures that makes Petya such an interesting character compared with the entire gallery of adult figures created by Kataev since the end of the 1920s. The author knows what it is to look at the world through Petya's eyes, and in typical fashion he does not spare the character, emphasizing his laziness, his vanity, and his slight vulgarity as well as his better qualities. Like the heroes of some stories of the 1920s, Petya attaches more importance to the immediate problems of life than to their wider context. But unlike those heroes, he does eventually arrive at an understanding of the relationship between private life and politics. Petya's dilemma was clearly of great personal importance to Kataev, and he returns to it in different forms in his other works of the 1960s. From all members of his class and generation, especially artists, life required a choice like Petya's. *Winter Wind* at least begins to explore this important theme, although Kataev oversimplifies the matter by making the Zarya-Zaryanitskys an unprincipled band of scoundrels and the Bolsheviks morally faultless.

In style, as well as in the character of its hero, *Winter Wind* represents a partial return to Kataev's manner of the 1920s. For the first time in over thirty years Kataev introduces fantasy through delirium, in such passages as the following: "He imagined that terrible word 'gangrene' as a long animal crawling along slowly, covered in black spots with yellowish-pink edges. And at the same time this animal was his numb thigh" (VI, 22).

One can conclude that at the beginning of the 1960s Kataev was again prepared to experiment a little (albeit very cautiously) in style, and to present a more complex picture than he had for many years of the central problem of his artistic life—his need to take sides in the revolutionary struggle.

CHAPTER 6

The "New" Kataev

ON completing the tetralogy which had occupied most of his creative energies for twenty years, Kataev entered a very productive period which has lasted until the present day and during which he has published seven long prose works and a short story. With the exception of the short story, entitled "Fialka" ("Violet," 1973), the works of this period all contain an openly autobiographical element, and in all of them chronology yields to association in the author's mind as the constructional principle. Most of the works of the 1960s and 1970s might be described as "memoirs," but Kataev has several times rejected this term and stressed that his recollections must not be taken as historically accurate. They are, he claims, a creative blend of fact, embellished fact, and fiction. As a token of his disregard for complete accuracy he refuses to verify his quotations, which are indeed not always reliable. In *My Diamond Crown* he writes about contemporaries such as Yury Olesha and Mikhail Bulgakov, but without naming them because he has no wish to be tied down to historical truth.

Of the many features that unify the works of the 1960s and 1970s the most important is the exploration of the many thousands of factors, both personal and suprapersonal, that have formed Kataev as he is today. In *The Grass of Oblivion* he recalls the two great influences on his work, Bunin and Mayakovsky; in *A Mosaic of Life* he recreates in great detail the atmosphere of his childhood (and, incidentally, presents as a persona a selfish and reckless fantast); *Kladbishche v Skulianakh (The Cemetery at Skulyany,* 1975) goes beyond his own lifetime to explore the lives of his ancestors and to view his life as part of a great chain; in *The Holy Well* he speaks in Aesopian language of the Stalinist years and the price of his survival. Time and again in all of the works from *Malen'kaia zheleznaia dver' v stene (The Little Iron Door in the Wall,* 1964) onwards, Kataev deals with the links between past and present—indeed he often deliberately confuses the two—so that his life emerges as the result of thousands of events and decisions, any one of which could have altered, ended, or even prevented it. Thus, among the many disparate themes of the work of this period, the fundamental one is that of self-exploration. As Kataev said in a speech in defense of young writers at the Third Congress of Soviet Writers in 1959: "Young authors most frequently write about themselves. Their theme is 'me and the world,' which is perfectly normal. Their primary need is to express themselves in art, because it is precisely this need—to speak about time and about oneself—that forms the essence of our writers' craft."[1] These words apply equally to his own later work.

I   The Little Iron Door in the Wall

The work thought by most critics to have heralded the arrival of the "new" Kataev was *The Holy Well*, but many of the themes and devices which were to run through Kataev's work for the rest of the 1960s and into the 1970s were introduced in a tale of 1964 about Lenin on Capri and in Paris, entitled *The Little Iron Door in the Wall*. Kataev defines the genre of this work as: "not a historical sketch, not a novel, not even a story. It is reflections, pages from travel notebooks, recollections; perhaps the best definition would be—a lyrical diary, no more. But no less" (IX, 7). The "lyrical diary" genre flourished in Soviet literature of the 1960s; among the best examples are Konstantin Paustovsky's *Story of a Life*, Ilya Ehrenburg's *People, Years, Life*, and Olga Berggolts's *Daytime Stars*. But Kataev's works of this period are distinguished from many other examples of the genre by their complexity and their inward focus. Kataev reveals more about himself than about Bunin and Mayakovsky in *The Grass of Oblivion*, fascinating though his pictures of the two poets are. Similarly, his picture of Lenin in *The Little Iron Door in the Wall* tells us less about the revolutionary leader than about the author's own tastes and interests.

The skeleton of the tale is provided by an account—based in part on the memoirs of contemporaries and in part on imagination—of Lenin's activities on Capri and in Paris. Although the work has no chapter divisions and displays little regard for conventional connected narrative, Lenin's life abroad is described by means of five major strands: his visits to Gorky's house on Capri; his daily bicycle journey across Paris to the library: his visits to the theater; his interest in aviation; and his friendship with the Lafargues. In addition, the historical associations of the Paris Commune are never far from Lenin's thoughts, and form a sixth element in his Parisian life.

However, although the figure of Lenin acts as a focal point for what narrative there is in the tale, Kataev's approach to the revolutionary leader is that of a contemporary, and while the point of view *appears* to be Lenin's, it in fact is Kataev's. It is no coincidence that the areas of Lenin's life imaginatively explored in the work are almost all areas in which the writer can share the leader's experiences. Kataev, too, knows Capri; he is fascinated by the architecture and topography of Paris; he loves its theaters; he recalls vividly his own excitement at the wonder of manned flight in the early years of the century. Thus, one may superimpose on the narrative skeleton another in which the central figure is the author, and which is purely digressive in spirit. The narrative and digressive structures fit closely together, flowing freely into each other as the tale progresses.[2]

Many of the paragraphs about Lenin are introduced by a phrase such as "I see" or "I can imagine," which enables the author to retain his central place. He never effaces himself. For example: "With astonishing clarity I can imagine an April morning on Capri, the jetty, and beyond it several tiers of pink, lilac, blue, pale yellow, and crimson houses, like a living mosaic . . ." (IX, 13). From his central position the author gives free rein to his eclectic tastes, often ascribing them to Lenin, as in the passage in which Lenin and Krupskaya watch, enthralled, as an airplane takes off. As Kataev admits:

How is it that I can so clearly imagine this typical Ile-de-France landscape in the summer of 1911; the hot breeze, the silky gleam of the clover field, the lilac-colored wrappers from Suchard Swiss chocolate lying discarded in the grass? . . . Probably because at that time almost everyone was fascinated by flying, and I myself, as a fourteen-year-old boy, would lie breathless with excitement among the wormwood, trying to catch that magic moment when the miracle of flight would take place before my eyes. [IX, 101]

Since his own personality, tastes, and memories stand at the center of the tale (albeit disguised by the figure of Lenin), Kataev may range as freely as he wishes, both in subject matter and in time, setting down incidents from various periods without regard to chronology. Several times he comments that time seems to stop for him, or to move backwards, and speaks of "the incomparable sweet sensation of the loss of time, or rather, its displacement. More and more often it pursues me now as I get older. I can see Capri as it was fifty years ago" (IX, 77). Kataev admits that the loss of a chronological sense comes with advancing years, but there is certainly no sign of senility in the resulting vivid descriptions of moments when time seems to stop.[3]

Even the work's strange title has to do with stopping time. In the most important scene the narrator (who may be taken to be Kataev) and his wife visit an aeronautical museum situated in a wood near Paris. The scene is at once realistic—it is brilliantly described—and symbolic. The little iron door in the wall opens to reveal, on the one hand, a museum of old aircraft and, on the other, the author's past. In stepping through the door he reverts to his own youth and recalls certain moments with such sensuous clarity that they appear to be taking place *now*.[4] Significantly, in the wood in which the museum with the iron door is situated Kataev half expects to meet Oberon with his magic horn (IX, 107), for Oberon possessed the ability to transport himself instantly to any place or time, a power that Kataev comes increasingly to claim for himself in his work of the 1960s and 1970s. In *A Mosaic of Life* he makes it clear that for him the figure of Oberon has come to symbolize the magic power of imagination and art.

The loss of a sense of time, which enables Kataev to bring together by association his childhood and his old age, assumes symbolic form in the figures of Luigi, a Capri boatman, and an old man at the museum. As a boy, Luigi had ferried Kataev and his father and brother into the Blue Grotto, and had also taken Lenin in his boat (an example of Kataev's method of ascribing his own experiences to Lenin). Fifty years later, on another visit to Capri, Kataev suddenly recognizes a boatman as the same Luigi, and is instantly transported to the Capri of 1910. Similarly, the old man at the museum becomes, in the author's imagination, the same man who had once worked as a mechanic at the aerodrome visited by Lenin fifty years earlier. Both Luigi and the old man act on Kataev's imagination in the same way as the frail aircraft, miraculously preserved through half a century of turbulent upheaval. They all serve to link past and present, to trigger artistic inspiration and that instantaneous flight into his past that is Kataev's equivalent of the magic of Oberon.

It is intriguing that this very personal subject matter should be woven into a tale that is ostensibly about Lenin. Lenin could easily be viewed as merely an excuse to make an experimental piece on personal themes more acceptable; but to do this would be to simplify what is probably a complex motivation. In 1958 Kataev had joined the Party formally, as he put it. By bringing together in this work a story about Lenin with a display of his own technical virtuosity and private reminiscences Kataev anticipates the theme of *The Grass of Oblivion*.

II *Mauvisme*

Kataev's literary experiments of the 1960s received a great deal of critical attention, partly because he coined a term—*mauvisme*—to describe them. However, the ideas on art that underlie *mauvisme* did not arise suddenly in the 1960s. They were all present or implied in a series of articles, written for the most part in the 1950s, in which Kataev makes four main points which sustain his literary theory and practice in the following two decades.

First, he stresses the need for formal innovation to suit new content. In an article of 1957 he defends the paintings of the avant-garde Suprematist group in the early 1920s on the grounds that these artists were responding to a new and revolutionary way of life by seeking new artistic forms, and goes on to advocate a general search for new forms, "for without constant renewal nothing can live, and this applies especially to art."[5] He makes it very clear that his call for formal innovation does not constitute a threat to Socialist Realism, which he interprets as sufficiently wide to absorb new forms. In a later article he tries to place his campaign for new forms firmly in the Communist tradition by recalling the innovatory role of the Party in all social spheres.[6]

Second, Kataev devotes a number of articles to the need for precise and detailed description which will capture the unique essence of material objects. It may well seem that there is nothing remotely revolutionary in such an appeal, but as one critic has recently reminded us, Socialist Realism eschewed specifics in favor of generalities, and this affected style.[7] Whereas the literature of the 1920s is full of precise, detailed descriptions, in later periods imprecise settings predominate.[8] Only in the Thaw period did particulars reappear to a substantial degree in Soviet literature. Kataev advises young authors to train themselves to isolate and express their first impressions.[9] Writers must learn to look at objects, however familiar, as if they were seeing them for the first time.

Kataev's third point concerns the musicality of prose. As early as 1940 he had written of the complex nature of the word, which, he said, contains visual, musical, and semantic elements.[10] By 1953 he was prepared to argue that the musical quality of language accounted for its most important artistic function: "Maupassant thought that the first thing a writer needs is vision. I consider that the first thing a writer needs is hearing. I repeat—the first thing he needs."[11]

Finally, in his articles on literature written in the 1950s Kataev stresses the centrality to all literary creation of the writer's personality. As with the second point above, this may appear so obvious as to be trite, but in the 1950s Soviet literature was only just beginning to emerge from a period of about twenty years when such individual features as whimsicality, stylistic eccentricity, and unusual vision had been suppressed. In one article Kataev claims for the author the right to interpret reality in the light of his own personality, rather than in a general way which would be identical for everyone: "an artist's consciousness must not be like a mirror, reflecting in the same way once and for all. The artist's consciousness must not only reflect, but also creatively transform the world. A writer bereft of imagination and fantasy ceases to be a true artist."[12]

The ideas expressed in these articles demonstrate that the Thaw enriched Soviet literature with a greater degree of artistic variety than had been possible for many years. But while Kataev's liberal views on art undoubtedly helped the many young writers whose works were published in *Yunost* under his editorship, the "new" approach to literature did not bear fruit in his own case until the middle of the 1960s when *The Holy Well* appeared and "the latest literary school—that of *mauvisme*" was founded, although, as we have seen, he made a cautious attempt to put some of these principles into practice with *The Little Iron Door in the Wall*.

Kataev supplied perhaps the most straightforward definition of *mauvisme* in a newspaper article of 1972: "It expresses the desire for new form."[13] The origin of the term is given in a passage from *The Holy Well* in which Kataev explains his new idea to his hostess at a cocktail party in Houston: "She was as pleased as a child, and even clapped her hands on learning that I was the founder of the latest literary school—the *mauvistes,* from the French *mauvais*—bad—the essence of which is that, since everyone nowadays writes very well, you must write badly, as badly as possible, and then you will attract attention" (IX, 223). There is a sarcastic note in this and other definitions of *mauvisme* which puts the reader on his guard, and to some extent it may even be dismissed as "a polemical joke," as Kataev himself calls it.[14] Yet the notion of writing "badly" is an important one which requires closer examination. When asked about his use of the words "badly" and "well" in this and similar passages, Kataev explained that he sought to write "badly" in the sense in which Matisse painted "badly." In an age when everyone painted "well," according to established canons, Matisse broke with those canons, and thereby expressed what he truly wanted to express.[15] Just as Kataev interprets Matisse's revolutionary style as a reaction to a tradition of painting which had become fossilized, so he sees his own intention to write "badly" as a reaction to the conventionality of Soviet prose, which he believes inhibits freedom of expression by imposing certain rules which must be followed without exception. In an interview he elaborated on this point by comparing the conventions of Soviet prose to a child's building bricks which can only be arranged in a limited number of ways.[16]

More than thirty years earlier, at the First Congress of Soviet Writers in 1934, Isaac Babel had also commented on bad writing. "Following Gorky," he remarked, "I would like to say that on our banner ought to be written Sobolev's [an earlier speaker] words that the Party and government have given us everything and have taken away only one right—the right to write badly. Comrades, let us not deceive ourselves. That was a very important right, and not a little is being taken away from us. It was a privilege which we used extensively."[17] Behind Babel's jocular tone lies a serious idea. If a writer agrees to any stricture on his artistic freedom from an external source, even if it is an apparently aesthetic stricture, then the way is open for the control of the writer by those external forces. In retrospect, it can be seen that Babel's apprehensions were well founded, for the history of Soviet literature since 1934 provides ample evidence that nonaesthetic criteria can become confused with aesthetic criteria, and that conventional writing can come to be regarded as the only good writing. In 1934 Soviet authors were called upon to give up the right to write badly, which led to the stifling of all formal innovation. Kataev's intention to write "badly" amounts to a rejection of the view that conventionality need necessarily be equated with high quality. It is in this sense that his joke of *mauvisme* is "polemical"—a polemic against Socialist Realist conventions.

Of course, the attempt to break free from convention is not peculiar to Soviet literature, and to the Western reader accustomed to French or English and American experimental prose, Kataev's *mauviste* works will scarcely appear exceptional. But in the context of a literature where formal innovation (especially in prose) was likely to bring down upon the author the serious charge of "formalism," and where the works of Marcel Proust and James Joyce had not been published or discussed openly for thirty years (after provoking interest and controversy in the 1920s and early 1930s), Kataev's unconventionality was a literary event of considerable significance.[18]

Of the accepted devices that Kataev rejects in his *mauviste* works the most important are plot and chronology, both of which are replaced by the personality and whims of the author. *The Holy Well* retains a tenuous link with conventional plot by means of dream sequences, but not so *Kubik*, where the author switches capriciously from one story line to another for no apparent reason other than his fancy and personal associations. By rejecting plot, or sustained illusion, Kataev focuses attention on the virtuoso aspect of his work. As in Olesha's *Not a Day Without a Line*—which undoubtedly influenced Kataev—the reader is not allowed to view the books as finished objects, but is brought into the workings of the author's mind, the initial ideas and visions which form his raw material.[19] In Mayakovsky-style, he even challenges the reader to do better (IX, 523–24).

An important aspect of Kataev's wish to reveal the unique personality of the author rather than hide it behind a screen of conventionality is his belief in the validity of the artist's first impressions, his inspiration at almost a preconscious level. Using the image of lightning for artistic inspiration, he says that "perhaps one of the main laws of *mauvisme* is to trace the silent precursor of the lightning" (IX, 495).

The other convention challenged by *mauvisme* is the use of chronology as an organizing principle. Kataev does not reject chronology out of hand, but he wants to show that it is merely one among several constructional possibilities, "simply a working hypothesis" (IX, 468).[20] In its place he puts association in his own memory, which enables him to jump back and forward in time, and also helps explain the conceit that he can see into the future.[21]

Kataev's works of the middle and late 1960s appear modernistic in the context of a tradition-bound Soviet prose, although he himself claims that he did not intend to bring down the edifice of Socialist Realism, but simply to point out that it could encompass modern forms. It is significant that in *The Holy Well* he implies a comparison between modern art and traffic signs, some of which are nonrepresentational but still have a utilitarian function (IX, 149). In other words, he apparently adheres to the view that art must serve a social function, but rejects the notion that this must necessarily be done through realistic and readily comprehensible form. In one of the key passages from *The Holy Well* he says:

[André] Maurois maintains that it is impossible to live simultaneously in two worlds—the real world and the world of the imagination—and that anyone who tries to do so will come to grief. I am convinced that Maurois is wrong. The person who comes to grief is the one who tries to live in only one of these two worlds. He is cheating himself, since he is denying himself exactly one half of the beauty and wisdom of life.

I have always lived in two dimensions. One without the other would be meaningless to me. Their separation would immediately turn art either into abstraction or into a trivial process of recording life. Only a blending of these two elements can create an art that is truly beautiful. Perhaps this is the essence of *mauvisme*. [IX, 204]

This is an unambiguous plea for the reintroduction of fantasy into Soviet literature, echoing the dissident critic and novelist Andrey Sinyavsky's view that the best way forward for that literature lies in a combination of realistic and fantastic elements.[22] Kataev takes pains to point out that what he advocates is not a completely new departure, but a return to the richness of the 1920s, when realism and fantasy, conventional and unconventional forms coexisted in Soviet literature.[23]

III   The Holy Well

Kataev submitted the manuscript of his first *mauviste*, or modernistic, work—*The Holy Well*—to the journal *Moskva* (*Moscow*), where it was accepted for publication, but then stopped at the last minute. Even an author of Kataev's seniority could hardly expect such a piece to appear in print without opposition; it contained many cryptic references to Stalin and to the servility of writers and others in the Stalin era. The tale was eventually published in slightly modified form in *Novy mir* in May 1966.

The Holy Well is a Felliniesque account of a reassessment of his life undertaken by Kataev in the early 1960s, following an operation and several journeys abroad to Europe and America. Waking at last after the long sleep of Stalinism, Kataev bemoans the loss of time and resolves to begin now what he could not do for so many years: write as he really wishes. In a passage near the beginning of the work the author both explains the literal meaning of the title (which also has a symbolic significance) and indicates that the tale will be about his own life: " 'The Holy Well' is the name of a small spring near the Peredelkino railway station on the Moscow-Kiev line where I thought out this book and pondered over my life" (IX, 147).[24]

A. *The Operation*

The narrator of *The Holy Well*[25] undergoes an operation, during which he has a number of dreams which form the basis of the tale. Throughout these dreams Kataev frequently returns to the reality of the operation, thus reminding the reader that the events described are visions induced by an anaesthetic. The operation provides a framework allowing for the introduction of fantasy and satire without the total abandonment of realism.

On one level the operation is performed by a surgeon, but on another it acquires symbolic significance through its connection with Pushkin's "The Prophet," lines from which are scattered through the text. Pushkin's poem on the nature of inspiration tells of a six-winged seraphim which pulls out the poet's "sinful tongue," cleaves open his breast, replaces his heart with a burning coal, and orders him to set alight the hearts of men with his words. Kataev quotes Pushkin's line "And he tore out my sinful tongue" at a particularly important point in the work, and thus seems to reject certain aspects of his previous work and look ahead to spiritual and artistic renewal.

As with the operation itself, the dreams are mostly based on real incidents from Kataev's life overlaid with a further level of significance. The sequence of dreams results from free association, one dream flowing into the next with a fluidity that had been lacking in Kataev's work since the 1920s. The style and tone alter suddenly as the mood of one dream gives way to the contrasting mood of another.

B. *"After Death"*

The first dream into which the anaesthetized narrator is plunged bears the title "After Death" (IX, 159). As it opens, he and his wife are sitting by the Holy Well near their home, watching an old man wash an endless supply of bottles. Kataev comments explicitly on this image: it represents eternity. "Eternity turned out to be not at all terrible and much easier to understand than we had previously thought" (IX, 146). The image of eternity as a well in which an endless stream of people are washed, each being returned after a moment to the sack whence he came, gives way later to a more orthodox materialist view in which eternity is seen as the way in which a stone turns to sand and then to a stone again while remaining the same matter (IX, 233). For all its apparent materialism, Kataev's philosophy of time and human life has certain points in common with Buddhism, and it is significant that in both *The Holy Well* and *The Grass of Oblivion* he makes several oblique references to that religion.[26]

After a brief section set in China, the narrator and his wife are transported in the dream to Normandy, where they settle down to a bucolic existence in a comfortable farmhouse resembling Kataev's own home in Peredelkino. Like Gogol's old-world landowners, their passionless lives revolve around food and drink and pass in contentment. With a cool, ironic detachment Kataev describes in detail this life of physical comfort, dwelling at length on the luxuries of the home: "Then I triumphantly threw open another door and showed them a magnificent ultra-modern bathroom with a cobalt-blue porcelain dressing table on one leg and a milk-white bath. The room was flooded with blindingly bright electric light; its tiles and nickel fittings sparkled; it was bedecked with soft, fragrant towels and sheets of pink and green and blue, and the floor was covered with rough coconut mats" (IX, 174).

The satire in this picture of a materialist heaven where all striving has ceased derives in part from the lushness of the descriptions, in part from the contrast between this scene and surrounding descriptions of the indignities and horrors of the Stalin era which create a grotesque framework for it. [27]

In his satirical dream of heaven as a well-appointed modern house Kataev questions the values that he and his contemporaries hold, although he knows himself well enough to realize that he will scarcely turn his back on material wealth.

C. *Osip Mandelshtam*

The first of the two dreams contrasting with the peaceful picture of heaven deals with Mandelshtam, whose fate was very different from Kataev's. The author narrows his focus to a particular incident which took place so long ago that it seems like a dream. He and Olesha "abduct" Nadezhda Mandelshtam, the poet's wife, and take her to a Georgian restaurant where they are later joined by Mandelshtam who recites a poem about Tiflis. [28] In passing, as it were, Kataev fires a shot at those who prevent Mandelshtam's poetry from being published in the Soviet Union. [29] After quoting some lines by the poet, he says: "And so on—you can check it and call it to mind again from a book of Mandelshtam's works, if you can get hold of one. I actually dreamt that—if you can get hold of one . . . ' " (IX, 160–61).

The full significance of the recurring dream about Mandelshtam emerges only when it is read in conjunction with subsequent dreams about a talking cat and the luxurious bathroom. Mandelshtam's presence may be felt in the background of *The Holy Well* and *The Grass of Oblivion* as an example of the uncompromising artist, one who refused to allow his words to be dictated by powerful people. He was no "talking cat" and never reaped the material benefit to which talking cats laid claim.

D. *The Talking Cat*

The dream about Mandelshtam shades almost imperceptibly into the surrealistic tale of a talking cat. The mention of Mandelshtam's poem about Georgia leads Kataev to recall a dream set in snowbound Tiflis. (Once again, one supposes, the "dream" is a distant memory of a real incident.) In the first section Kataev paints a satirical picture of a hack writer who accompanies him to Georgia, possibly as his "watchdog." This hated companion, called Prokhindeykin, is "a modification of Faddey Bulgarin" (IX, 169). Bulgarin was a contemporary of Pushkin's generally thought to be a police spy; Prokhindeykin may thus represent a writer turned informer for the secret police. Abject as the lickspittle Prokhindeykin is, he serves as a mere introduction to a more powerful image of the conformism of terrified writers during the Stalin era. At a party in Georgia the host entertains his guests with a cat that says *mama* and *maman* in Russian and French when two fingers are inserted in its throat. It eventually dies while trying to pronounce the word "neocolonialism." In a cryptic reference to the purges of the 1930s Kataev compares the cat to a gladiator and the host to Caesar: "The cat—younger brother to the tiger—walked like a gladiator around the feast table and stopped near the host, as if wishing to exclaim: '*Ave Caesar, morituri te salutant!*' " (IX, 166)

This transparent fable reveals such a vehement degree of self-disgust and hatred for Stalin that it is no surprise to learn that in 1966 Kataev was one of the twenty-five intellectuals—including Maya Plisetskaya, Andrey Sakharov, and Viktor Nekrasov—who signed a letter to Leonid Brezhnev warning against any rehabilitation of Stalin.[30]

E. *The Journey to America*

The major part of *The Holy Well* deals with the narrator's journey to America. The description of the transatlantic flight, which occupies several pages, contains numerous references to the disorientation in time experienced by the air-traveler. Beyond their literal meaning, these comments on time are linked with the whole question of Kataev's spiritual reassessment. It subsequently emerges that the narrator goes to America partly to meet again a lady with whom he had been in love before the Revolution and who had emigrated. In other words, the journey to America represents a journey back to his youth; aside from its literal meaning, the flight can be seen as a metaphor for the narrator's exploratory journey into his past. Its function, then, is similar to that of the anaesthetic during the operation.

Many episodes in *The Holy Well* and *The Grass of Oblivion* operate in a dual manner, on the realistic and symbolic levels. The clearest expression of the relationship between life and art in these works occurs in *The Grass of Oblivion,* where Kataev says: "and life, having become for a moment a page of Hugo, went on its way again" (IX, 326). At odd moments in the course of a lifetime, then, life rises to the level of art. Events that may appear at the time to blend perfectly into the natural flow of life later appear exceptional, like episodes in a novel.[31] In the light of hindsight, these moments stand out from their contexts and assume a symbolic value. In *The Holy Well* such moments include the instant when, as a young boy, Kataev fell in love with the girl who later emigrated; the evening spent in the restaurant with Olesha and the Mandelshtams; and the flight to America.

A similar principle operates in the shoeshine episode, which begins before the flight and fills many pages after the narrator has arrived in America. At first the narrator's concern lest the state of his shoes embarrass him in a foreign country appears to be a purely ironical detail, satirizing the sense of inferiority felt by Soviet tourists in the West. But as he returns time and again with increasing compulsion to the state of his shoes—a crescendo which culminates in a mock-tragic encounter with a New York shoeshine boy—the comic detail takes on a serious aspect. Such manic compulsiveness had appeared before in Kataev's work, for example in "The Father," where concentration on a trivial detail (picking up paper while not moving the feet) served to convey a character's deep fear of impending death. The shoeshine incident, too, is symbolic of the passing of time and the approach of death. (On the flight itself only the gradual dulling of the shoes conveys the passing of time.) Thus, a single detail serves a double function—the one comic and satirical, the other serious and philosophical. A slight misadventure which, in all probability, really befell Kataev in New York, assumes several meanings, and is described in a number of different styles.

A recurrent theme in *The Holy Well*, particularly the American section, is that of nuclear war. On the journey to America three of the narrator's fellow-passengers wear the uniforms of the Spearhead forces in charge of the United States' atomic weaponry. Later Kataev refers to submarines carrying atomic rockets and to an underground atomic explosion in Nevada that he detected only through its effect on the rate of his heartbeat. Finally, he makes many references to burning, charring, and carbonizing, often in strangely incongruous contexts. For example, on a hot day in Moscow the narrator and his family appear to be about to burst into flames: "At the time we could hardly bear this airlessness, this terrible, indescribable heat which seemed to come from somewhere like Hiroshima. It even seemed that our clothes were starting to carbonize" (IX, 157). In another example the narrator sees himself as a winged creature (the connection with Pushkin's "The Prophet" has already been pointed out), but his wings are "charred" and "incinerated" (IX, 239, 242). One of the Spearhead men hides his "dark, almost carbonized face" (IX, 178). When the American dream ends and the narrator gradually emerges from his state of unconsciousness, his last dream is of an atomic explosion and the disintegration of matter, which gradually merges into the reality of the hospital bed, the bottle of blood, and the oxygen tubes in his nostrils.[32]

It is difficult to grasp the precise significance of the many references to nuclear war in *The Holy Well*. If they are interpreted literally, Kataev is warning about the possibility of total destruction, which may be averted through sensible action. In this respect his book resembles the traffic signs he so frequently mentions: it looks into the future and warns of a hazard. It is possible, however, that in addition the references to burning are a metaphor for Stalinism, which may well have appeared renascent in the mid-1960s.

Kataev's attitude toward the achievements of American technology and the sophistication of the American way of life is ambivalent. On the one hand, he satirizes excessive American automation (his "fight" with a fully automated hotel room in Houston is one of the funniest scenes in the book); on the other hand, like Mayakovsky before him, he freely expresses his awe at the scale and beauty of American technological achievement: "we flew like a fly through the middle of a huge harp with white strings" (IX, 195), he says of the George Washington bridge.

Kataev offers some harsh and unsubtle comments on racial tensions in the United States, but he reserves his most effective satire for his fellow-countrymen abroad. In New York he meets a Soviet diplomat, Alfred Parasyuk, who brings to mind the horrible bootlicking timeserver Prokhindeykin and the talking cat. The story of Parasyuk's social blunder at the Waldorf Astoria ranks with the best of Kataev's satire, and makes very clear his view of his boorish compatriots in official positions abroad. Parasyuk tells the story and condemns himself through his very style of speech (a common satirical device, known in Russian as *skaz*). He is a smart dresser whose proud boast is that "you could take me for a foreigner, couldn't you?" (IX, 196) However, his campaign to appear as sophisticated as any Westerner is thwarted by a "provocation" at an official luncheon.

The lunch is finishing and the waiters in white silk stockings bring crystal finger-bowls. Now you know, I've been caught that way before. I wasn't born yesterday. I know what's what. I'm an educated man. I've read the official instructions. If after a lunch they bring you a bowl, then for heaven's sake don't drink it, because it's not lemonade, it's for rinsing your fingers. Some of our lads have come a real cropper on that one, but not me. I take the bowl and start to wash my hands for all to see. Only it turns out to be a pineapple compote. Just imagine! In front of the entire Waldorf Astoria I washed my hands in a pineapple compote. And it even turned a bit blue, sort of purplish. [IX, 197][33]

F. *The Russian Widow*

Toward the end of the work Kataev turns to the motif of the emigré Russian lady, now a widow, whom he had loved when both were adolescents in Odessa. The dramatist Viktor Rozov, who accompanied Kataev to the United States, has confirmed that this meeting with an old friend really did take place, and that it meant a great deal to Kataev:

If I had the gift of writing prose I would write a story about the author himself [Kataev] whom I observed at this time. How he looked forward to this meeting while we were still in Moscow, how the impending meeting occupied him more and more the closer we came to San Francisco, and how he talked of it more and more frequently. He seemed to grow slimmer with every hour. How on the day of the meeting he was triumphant . . . And how he came back from the meeting devastated, limp, tragic.[34]

With great tenderness the narrator recalls an Easter day many years before when he had kissed the girl who is now this widow. Though it was not apparent at the time, that had in fact been one of the decisive moments of his life. The real incident of the meeting with the Russian widow acquires symbolic overtones, for she represents a part of Kataev's personality which turns to the West. At least two people whom he loved (this woman and Bunin) had emigrated, and in the 1960s Kataev dealt several times with the theme of emigration. Ultimately, of course, he has no doubt that his decision to remain in Russia was correct, but in both *The Holy Well* and *The Grass of Oblivion* he shows that the need to choose caused a split within himself, and that something was irretrievably lost.[35] Significantly, of the several expressions of love for his homeland in *The Holy Well* the most eloquent and moving one occurs in the section about the Russian widow. He affirms his love for Russia despite her faults and the heartache she has caused him. The passage is too long to quote in full, but its final few lines read:

One could guess at the existence among the fields, meadows, and forests, of chemical factories, space-centers, and the criss-cross catapults of the high-voltage pylons striding in all directions across the unique, inimitable, thrice-blessed land of my soul, which has given me so much joy, so many emotional heights and depths, moments of disillusionment and intense happiness, elevated thoughts, important and petty affairs, love and hatred, sometimes despair . . . . [IX, 235]

As Kataev has recently admitted, his decision to remain in Russia and support the Revolution was not an easy one.[36] But now he does have his homeland, whereas the widow does not (and neither does the Bunin of *The Grass of Oblivion*). The widow's last words to the narrator are: "I no longer have anyone here. No one in the world. I can live quite comfortably, but I have been left totally alone" (IX, 241).

Having traveled to America to see this woman, the narrator appears to have done much to heal his own wound by overcoming his fascination with her. Reality has replaced his idealized picture. The meeting has drained him, but also left him convinced of the rightness of his decision to remain in Russia. He feels like a man who has dived to a great depth to bring up the marble statue of a goddess from the seabed and has found instead a little blackened terracotta statuette of a widow (IX, 243). In view of the widow's partially symbolic nature, Kataev appears to be saying here that his trip to America helped him to understand better the nature of the split within himself and reinforced his conviction that he had taken the correct path.

The most notable feature of the style of *The Holy Well* is the length and density of its sentences. Many are of paragraph length, with clauses branching out at almost every conceivable point and with detail piled upon detail.

And I, an emigrant from an entirely different world who, as it were, found himself in a zone of spiritual weightlessness, seemed to float in my reclining chair somewhere at the intersection of day and night, and having finished my grapefruit and the huge toasted tinned ham and processed cheese sandwiches garnished with damp lettuce leaves and covered with squiggles of mayonnaise—I already held in my hand a ridiculously weightless plastic cup, into which an air hostess with bleached hair and wearing a sexy uniform poured over my shoulder from a thermos jug a thick stream of mocha, heavy as gold, above which hung a divinely bitter steam. [IX, 200]

This typical sentence illustrates the way in which many nouns are qualified by one or more adjectives, which are themselves modified by an adverb expressing the author's attitude toward the adjectives. Thus, the steam is "bitter," and the bitterness is "divine"; or the cup is weightless, and its weightlessness is "ridiculous."

This style owes little or nothing to the spoken language, and in fact it is almost impossible to read Kataev's sentences aloud. In this respect it resembles Bunin's mature style, as one critic has pointed out: "Many of the pages in the later works of V. Kataev look like an obvious stylization of Bunin's prose."[37] But the style of *The Holy Well* and the other works of the 1960s follows the Bunin tradition only in certain respects. In others it is totally different. (This point must be emphasized because Kataev's repeated reminders throughout the 1960s that Bunin was his teacher might lead to an exaggerated view of the influence of Bunin's style upon him.) The vivid description of physical objects, making them appear almost tangible (referred to in *The Grass of Oblivion* as "stereoscopic description"), is certainly in the Bunin tradition, as are certain syntactic features. But in the 1920s Kataev had favored a bolder, more extravagant style which came to be known as Southern Russian,[38] and this, too, forms part of the style of the 1960s. For example, the fantastic images of "Sir Henry and the Devil" are far from the Bunin tradition, but they are just as important in the formation of the "new" Kataev's style.

The Holy Well is not an easy book to read. In addition to its deliberately tortuous syntax, it contains a number of unglossed foreign words and many references to other authors, to composers, artists, and film-makers (for example, Fellini, whose wife and leading actress, Giuletta Masina, the narrator meets in his dream about heaven). Toward the end of the work Kataev helps to explain this aspect of *The Holy Well* when he remarks that it is "a book for the few" (IX, 240). Whereas he had earlier written for a mass readership, he now addresses himself unashamedly to the relatively few people able to understand his references. And this is very distant from the Socialist Realist view of literature, however much Kataev may protest that he has not departed from it. His intellectual and cultural elitism is part of *mauvisme,* and he would go even further along this path with *Kubik.*

IV   The Grass of Oblivion

In an interview of 1962 Kataev identified Bunin and Mayakovsky as the greatest influences on him.[39] Two years later he began work on *The Grass of Oblivion,* a book which is, on one level, a memoir about those two poets—like Ehrenburg's *People, Years, Life* and Fedin's *Gorky Among Us*—but which has Kataev's own literary development as its principal theme.

The structure of *The Grass of Oblivion* supports the contention that the author's focus is primarily inward. Though lacking formal divisions, the work consists of two major sections devoted to Bunin and Mayakovsky respectively, with a link passage about a misadventure that befell Kataev during the Civil War, and a final brief section that returns to Bunin. In addition, the author turns several times to the story of Klavdiya Zaremba, the girl from the Party school, who binds together Bunin, Mayakovsky, and Kataev himself. Thus, while at first sight *The Grass of Oblivion* appears to consist of two parts about the two poets, its structure is quite complex and is held together, not by the ostensible subjects, but by the figure of Kataev. Both Bunin and Mayakovsky are depicted almost exclusively in relation to Kataev, and he neglects several important aspects of the work and personalities of the poets in favor of those aspects that affected him.[40] The aim of *The Grass of Oblivion* is to explore the apparent paradox of the influence on Kataev of two such different, indeed antithetical, writers as Bunin and Mayakovsky. In so doing, Kataev presents a superb portrait of Bunin and a very interesting picture of Mayakovsky in the last years of his life

A. *"Stereoscopic" Description and Its Limitations*

Until he read Bunin's poetry, Kataev's own verses had been full of conventional descriptions inspired more by literary models (Afanasy Fet, Mikhail Lermontov, Valery Bryusov and others) than by any actual experience. But a poem by Bunin which compares a seagull floating on the water to a fisherman's float suddenly revealed to him "the simple secret of poetry"—the fact that a poem could be full of concrete details of everyday physical objects, which would appear before the reader with astonishing clarity, as if he were observing them for the first time. Kataev terms Bunin's description of the seagull "stereoscopic" because of the extraordinary impression of depth and solidity with which it conveyed the subject to him. It became an ideal toward which he strove all his life.

At about the same time he first read Bunin's poem, Kataev read something by another poet which also opened his eyes to "the simple secret of poetry." That was Mayakovsky's "Port" ("The Port"), and in particular the line "The anchor-earrings glittered in the ears of deafened steamers." Although just then he did not even remember the name of the Futurist poet who had written the line, the image of the port remained in his memory alongside Bunin's description of the floating seagull (IX, 275).

The fact that both Bunin and Mayakovsky taught Kataev an aesthetic lesson, that both were capable of "stereoscopic description," shows that true artistry is compatible with an ideologically committed stance, at least for a poet of Mayakovsky's stature. If Kataev did not mention the aesthetic impact of the latter's poetry, the figures of Bunin and Mayakovsky might be interpreted as symbolizing artistry on the one hand and ideological commitment on the other. But in *The Grass of Oblivion* Bunin has no monopoly on poetic artistry, although it is undeniable that the stereoscopic vision which so thrilled Kataev belongs, above all, to him, and that the major lesson Kataev learned from Mayakovsky was ideological.

In the course of his recollections of Bunin in the early part of the work Kataev attempts to define the essence of the latter's descriptive powers: "Bunin's strength as a descriptive writer consisted in his amazingly rapid, almost instantaneous reaction to all external stimuli and his ability to find for them an immediate and completely accurate verbal expression" (IX, 309). It is interesting to note that in his work of the 1960s Kataev strives to emulate this aspect of Bunin's writing. Time after time in *The Holy Well*, *The Grass of Oblivion*, and *Kubik*, he speaks of reacting to stimuli from the physical world around him; for example when he says at one point: "My soul is constantly assailed from outside by millions of perceptible and imperceptible stimuli which suddenly begin to demand with a terrible insistence that I give them a material three-dimensional body" (IX, 371).

As Bunin's pupil, Kataev also mastered the art of instantly finding the right words to depict a person or object with a few telling details, as, for example, in his first description of Vera Nikolaevna, Bunin's wife (IX, 281). Although he professes to love Bunin, he does not allow that to affect his description of him or his wife, which is dispassionate. He approaches the description of Bunin and Vera Nikolaevna as he would any other person or object, that is, with curiosity and a determination to find the right words. It is a puzzling feature of *The Grass of Oblivion* that whereas, toward the end of the book, Kataev criticizes Bunin's work as mere imaginative gymnastics, a pure exercise in verbal skill (a criticism that will surely be shared by few of Bunin's readers), he himself imitates, or perhaps even parodies, Bunin's search for the right word. In order to demonstrate Bunin's coldly accurate approach, Kataev quotes the following passage from his *Lika:* "I hold my head back until it becomes painful. I keep staring at [the moon], and as it suddenly emerges, shining, from some clouds, I keep on trying to work out what it is like. A white death-mask, perhaps? It is glowing from within, but what is it like? Stearin? Yes, yes, stearin! I'll use that somewhere!" (IX, 432)[41]

A few pages after this passage, Kataev depicts himself as a similarly dispassionate seeker after accurate comparisons, when with callous lack of feeling he searches for a word to capture the essence of Bunin's aged widow, whom he meets in Paris. "I looked at her with the same agitated attention with which the young Bunin had once looked at the moon, trying to define as accurately as possible what it was like. Stearin? I think I have found a comparison for the whiteness which dominated everything in Vera Nikolaevna's face. It was the color of a white mouse with pink eyes" (IX, 436). It seems likely that the reference to the white mouse is a deliberately stylized imitation of Bunin. In juxtaposing such an unfeeling description of Vera Nikolaevna with Bunin's own description of the moon as "stearin," Kataev apparently questions the morality of Bunin's commitment to dispassionate description. Yet, despite the attempt to involve Bunin through the juxtaposition, the comparison of Vera Nikolaevna to a white mouse still belongs to Kataev, and it is difficult not to conclude that he has sacrificed some human feeling in his search for accuracy of description.

Kataev admires Bunin's descriptive power, and throughout the

1960s he continues to try to emulate the great writer's "stereoscopic" vision. Yet he has reservations about him, and believes that the great limitation of his work is the absence of "external moral pressure" (IX, 433). Lacking a belief or an ideology, Bunin cannot cope with what Goethe calls "the thousand-headed hydra of empiricism." Bunin's problem, we recall, resembles that of Georgy Vasilevich in *Time, Forward!* before he was supplied with the key to the rebus. Similarly, Kataev suggests in *The Grass of Oblivion* that he himself was saved from "the hydra of empiricism" by his support for the Revolution, and attributes to Mayakovsky an important role in his transformation, since "it was Mayakovsky who taught me the Revolution" (IX, 432). At another point he writes: "I am a son of the Revolution. A bad son, perhaps, but nevertheless a son" (IX, 331).

Thus, "stereoscopic description"—the ability to describe physical objects in such a way that they appear solid and three-dimensional—remains as much of an ideal for Kataev in the 1960s as when Bunin's magic first thrilled him. His own descriptive writing in all the works of the 1960s is of a very high standard (although it must be said that, unlike Bunin, Kataev seems to revel in his ability to describe objects for its own sake). However, in *The Grass of Oblivion* he claims that descriptive powers must be allied to the political commitment of a Mayakovsky.

B. *Ryurik Pchelkin and Klavdiya Zaremba*

Kataev appears in *The Grass of Oblivion* both as mature narrator, writing in the 1960s, and as youthful autobiographical hero, living through turbulent events in the period of Revolution and Civil War. He is clearly aware of the differences between these two personas, and he maintains a subtle distinction in perception and language between himself when young and himself now, which does much to account for the complexity of Bunin's portrait, and to a lesser extent Mayakovsky's. For example, in describing Bunin, Kataev mixes the observations of the acute but naive autobiographical hero with the reflections of the experienced, elderly narrator, who enjoys the advantage of historical perspective. Consequently, the hero's admiration for the great writer emerges, but is constantly accompanied by the narrator's knowledge of Bunin's future path and tragic fate.[42]

At an important point in the narrative the author acknowledges the distinction he has been maintaining between his two personas and sharpens it by giving his autobiographical hero a different name, Ryurik Pchelkin. "This young man—who still looked a mere youth—was me. Or rather, he could be me if I had the power to resurrect myself as I was when a young man in those far-off days" (IX, 341).

Pchelkin, a young Odessan poet, is sent to the outlying rural districts to recruit correspondents for his newspaper. Though he carries out his duties conscientiously, he is really most interested in poetry—his own and that of Bunin and Mandelshtam. As his mission is nearing an end, he falls into the hands of a terrorist band and is lucky to escape with his life, unlike his traveling companion, who is executed. A false report of Pchelkin's death reaches Odessa and his father, on hearing it, suffers a fatal stroke.

The story accords with that published in Kataev's 1959 autobiography, and also, in most respects, with the story of Petr Sinaysky in "The Father." The significance of its position at the center of *The Grass of Oblivion* lies in the fact that Pchelkin is a poet, an admirer and pupil of Bunin, who spends much of his time composing verses or reciting those of other poets. Yet he is also working for the Revolution, and in this respect he bears a closer resemblance to Mayakovsky than to Bunin.

A similar indication of Kataev's position midway between Bunin and Mayakovsky is provided by the story of Klavdiya Zaremba, the girl from the Party school. Significantly, it is Bunin who first encourages Kataev to describe the girl when he tells him to describe a sparrow in a way which will express his own feelings rather than repeat those of any other writer, however great. Kataev, in the person of the autobiographical hero, tries to act on Bunin's advice. After describing the sparrow, he seeks to describe a little girl in the same way. But he feels that in her there is something that demands to be expressed, not by exquisite lyric poetry, but by an epic or a tragedy: "With all my soul I suddenly felt in her not simply a girl, but the tragic heroine of some real rather than fictional, ripening future novel" (IX, 271). The girl whom Kataev tried to describe in a poem in response to Bunin's instruction turned out to be Klavdiya Zaremba, the tragic heroine of a novel that Kataev longed all his life to write, but never did. "Describe a sparrow," said Bunin, and as a result Kataev was led to the figure of Klavdiya Zaremba, who could not simply be described, for in her, landscape demanded to be turned into "epic, into tragedy" (IX, 271).

Kataev's other teacher, Mayakovsky, also led him to the figure of Klavdiya Zaremba, for he gave him the title for his novel about Magnitogorsk, and Zaremba turned up in that town while Kataev was collecting the material for *Time, Forward!* Thus, the advice from two completely antithetical poets brought Kataev from different points to the central figure of Klavdiya Zaremba.

The story of Zaremba is based on a real incident. When Kataev was working for ROSTA in the early 1920s the editor was a Bolshevik named Sergey Ingulov. In the autumn of 1921 Ingulov published a cycle of sketches about the effect of the Revolution on the lives of individuals. One of them, "The Girl from the Party School,"[43] told the story of a girl who, acting on the instructions of the Cheka, had befriended and then fallen in love with a counter-revolutionary agent. When she had gathered information against him, he was arrested and shot. She had sacrificed her love for the sake of the Revolution. Ingulov urged writers to seek inspiration from such incidents from Soviet life.

In Ingulov's article the girl from the Party school was not named, but Kataev calls her Klavdiya Zaremba, transforming her from a real person into a creature of his imagination. Like the Russian widow in *The Holy Well*, Zaremba is an example of real life's rising to the level of art. She becomes a symbolic figure whose fate is bound up with Kataev's own. The fact that the author has invented her name assumes considerable importance, for it epitomizes his relationship to his work. The ant which crawls over a flower and onto his arm reacts to the various stimuli surrounding it, but because it has neither imagination nor the ability to confer names it differs from the author (IX, 370). He too reacts to the stimuli from the world around him, but then he converts that experience into art.

Such a view of the nature of artistic creativity accords perfectly with the passage from *The Holy Well* in which Kataev takes issue with Maurois. According to this view, an author needs descriptive powers and imagination in equal measure; his work should be based on reality, but should also contain an element of fantasy to express his uniqueness. Thus, the girl from the Party school really existed, and her story so moved Kataev that it demanded to be given artistic form. It provided the external stimulus. But his artistic vision transformed the facts. Kataev emphasizes the degree of his control over his character by discussing his deliberations over the choice of name, and by making it such an unusual one: "At last I myself gave her a name: Klavdiya Zaremba. Yes, just so: Klavdiya Zaremba. Or Zarembo?" (IX, 370).

C. *The Angel of Death*

The story of Klavdiya Zaremba and Petya Solovev, the White agent with whom she falls in love and whom she betrays to the Cheka, should have formed the subject matter of a novel entitled *The Angel of Death* which Kataev wished to write, and to which he turned many times, but which, in the end, he could not create. *The Grass of Oblivion* is, in part, an adumbration of that unwritten novel. Kataev addresses himself to the question of why the "book of his dreams" remained unwritten: "How many times have I taken up my pen in order to . . . write a novel about the girl from the Party school. . . . But each time I was aware of my lack of power. The subject was many times greater than I . . . The girl from the Party school would have to be written about in a completely new and unprecedented way, as my friend Osip Mandelshtam would say 'fit to burst the aorta.' And I was not yet ready for that" (IX, 378–79).

We must ask why this subject, which appears no more extraordinary than many others in Soviet literature, was so demanding for the author? A possible answer to this question emerges from the fact that when, at last, Kataev did write about the girl who betrayed her lover because of her greater love for the Revolution, he did so within a book devoted mainly to his own relationship to Bunin and Mayakovsky. It is tempting to suppose that the story of Klavdiya Zaremba so moved Kataev because he saw in it a parallel to his own treatment of Bunin. By a curious coincidence, Ingulov's article "The Girl from the Party School" appeared in the same issue of the Kharkov newspaper *Kommunist* (*Communist*) in which Kataev's satirical story about Bunin—"The Gold Nib"—was first published. For Kataev the writing of "The Gold Nib" was equivalent to Zaremba's sacrifice of her lover for the cause of the Revolution. Just as she never ceases to love Petya Solovev even after betraying him, so does Kataev: "I continued to love [Bunin] passionately. I do not want to add 'as an artist.' I loved him fully, as a man as well, as an individual" (IX, 327). Or again: "Without exaggeration I can say that my whole life has been permeated by the desire to see Bunin again, even just once" (IX, 429).

The ambiguity of the relationship between Klavdiya Zaremba and

Petya Solovev resembles that of the connection between Kataev
and Bunin as presented in *The Grass of Oblivion*. Thus, alongside
Klavdiya's abiding love for Petya there is her recognition of a greater
love for the Revolution, and her ability to see Petya's attitude as
treachery. Kataev has her write shortly before her death: "You are
the only one that I'll admit it to before I die—I loved him and have
never for a moment forgotten him all my life. You know who I am
talking about. But my conscience is clear, both with regard to our
Revolution and myself. It was not I who betrayed him, but he who
betrayed his country" (IX, 441). Similarly, Kataev professes his love
for Bunin, but at the same time justifies his own betrayal of him by
depicting the great author as an Esau who sold his birthright for a
mess of pottage. Toward the end of *The Grass of Oblivion* he writes:
"I realized that Bunin had exchanged the two most valuable things
of all—Homeland and Revolution—for a mess of pottage of so-called
freedom and so-called independence" (IX, 431).[44]

When Kataev at last goes to Paris to see Bunin's grave, he meets
Petya Solovev, who has escaped execution and lived in emigration
for many years. Now, in his old age, he works as a cemetery at-
tendant at the Orthodox cemetery where Bunin is buried. In this
closeness there is a hint that the banality and unhappiness of Solovev's life as an emigré were shared by Bunin. Kataev's attempt
in the later pages of *The Grass of Oblivion* to present Bunin's life
in Paris as one of poverty and squalor has been severely criticized
by those who knew the Bunin family in Paris and, interestingly
enough, by Soviet scholars as well.[45] Kataev's distortion of the facts
may be at least understood, if not excused, if the Paris scenes are
interpreted as forming part of the process of self-justification undertaken through the story of Klavdiya Zaremba. The tragic fates
of Zaremba and Petya Solovev and the squalid picture of Bunin's
Paris flat buttress one of the main themes of Kataev's later work:
that he had been correct in his decision to remain in Russia and to
continue to write, despite all the constraints which that decision
implied.

V   Kubik

While Kataev frequently asserts in his work of the 1960s that he
is a Soviet author, "a son of the Revolution," the fundamental tenor
of all his writings of this period is aesthetic rather than hortatory,

private rather than public. *The Little Iron Door in the Wall, The Holy Well,* and *The Grass of Oblivion* are unified (both individually and as a group) by the figure of the author, which is never far from the foreground. This tendency culminates in his last tale of the 1960s, *Kubik,* published in February 1969.

Kubik appears to have been originally envisaged as a tale for children, and the early pages lead the reader to believe that in it Kataev has returned to the style of *Lone White Sail.*[46] Also, certain details echo the earlier work. But it very quickly becomes clear that this similarity is merely superficial.

Kubik opens with a tale about a boy and girl in pre-revolutionary Odessa. The boy is an autobiographical figure. "Can that boy really be me as well? If not completely, then at least partly. It could be that he is that same Pchelkin who is dear to my heart, only quite small, about eight years old" (IX, 451). Young Ryurik Pchelkin and his friend Sanya find the letters OV chalked in various places in the city, and invent adventure stories to account for them. But, just as the tale gathers momentum, Sanya drowns, and the narrative switches to a completely different track. Young Pchelkin becomes Monsieur the Former Boy, a rich French businessman of Russian origin (once again the theme of emigration), who returns to Odessa as a tourist and discovers that the letters OV which had so fascinated him as a boy stand for nothing more exotic than the Russian words for "Odessa Waterworks." The tale then shifts once more to encompass a love story in the style of Maupassant, in which Monsieur the Former Boy conducts an affair with a poor but handsome woman, who is struggling to bring up her only daughter decently. After her sudden death at an early age the story switches to the daughter's wedding and her honeymoon in Bulgaria and Rumania. (Kataev here uses the technique he had introduced in *The Little Iron Door in the Wall* of accompanying his heroes to places that he himself knows well, describing those places from his own point of view, and then ascribing similar experiences to his heroes.)

After the death of his mistress, Monsieur the Former Boy seeks solace in travel and, among other places, visits East Germany. This gives Kataev an excuse to describe his own visits to that country, and to incorporate the famous story of Luther's throwing an inkwell at the Devil, which is important for his underlying theme.

Next the scene shifts to Monte Carlo, where Monsieur and Madame are spending a holiday. During a strike of power workers, their dog, Kubik, bites a Corsican waiter named Napoleon. The latter allows himself to be placated cheaply, and then bitterly regrets his inability to obtain a larger sum in compensation.

The tale ends in Paris during a period of social unrest, probably the disturbances of May 1968. Napoleon, enraged and embittered by his failure to seize his opportunity for enrichment, becomes involved with criminals and sinks slowly into drunkenness and squalor. Monsieur goes down to his cellar for a bottle of mineral water and suffers a stroke or heart attack, during which he sees again the letters OV which had earlier fascinated him.

A. *Intonation, Sound, and the "Effect of Presence"*

This account of the main episodes in *Kubik* demonstrates that the tale has no unifying plot, and even the figure of Monsieur the Former Boy unifies it only in a very general sense. A clue to the principle of the work's construction comes at the end, when Kataev calls it "not a tale, not a novel, not a sketch, not travel notes, but simply a bassoon solo with orchestral accompaniment . . ." (IX, 536). The work may be compared to a modern musical composition in which each separate section has its own key and its own rhythm. In *Kubik* Kataev develops more fully than ever before the thoughts about the sound of prose which he had first advanced in his article of 1953 entitled "Novogodnii tost" ("A New Year's Toast"). He had long been regarded as an expert judge of painting, whose work could be compared to that of an artist like Albert Marquet,[47] but in *Kubik*, while still revealing his painterly qualities, he emphasizes the musical aspect of his prose. It is highly significant that at one point Kataev quotes Mandelshtam—to whom he is indebted for much in *Kubik*—as saying, " 'prose is asymmetrical; its movement— the movement of a mass of words—is herd movement, complex and rhythmic in its irregularity; real prose is dissonance, discord, polyphony, counterpoint . . . ' " (IX, 483).

Each major section of *Kubik* has its own intonation, and formal division into chapters is replaced by skillful variations in pace and tone.[48] In general, Kataev does not switch suddenly and irrevocably from one intonation to another, but uses a contrapuntal method, interrupting a section with a passage written in a different style— a different "musical key"—which is then developed fully in the succeeding section. Thus the entire work moves forward in counterpoint. For example, the opening section is, for the most part, a simple narrative, written in short paragraphs and making extensive use of dialogue. But in the middle of this section Kataev introduces a long paragraph that anticipates the theme and style of a later section and contrasts strikingly with the predominant tone of the surrounding passage (IX, 455–56).

If musical sound, or intonation, is important in *Kubik*, then non-musical sound is no less so. In distinguishing between sound and intonation, Kataev says of the former: "Sound is something quite different . . . It is always some secret information, a source of signals which, as it were, model the thing making the sound in world space. The magic 'effect of presence.' . . . Sound is the consciousness of quivering matter" (IX, 455). Objects emit "sound" which is picked up by poets, who then recreate the objects, or establish "the magic effect of presence," by finding the right words. (It is worth noting, in passing, that scientific imagery, in particular connected with the reception of signals from space, is characteristic of Kataev's work at this time.) The author links his concept of sound to that of artistic creativity by his use of the term "the magic effect of presence," which he will apply later to modern poetry. For the development of his ideas on sound and "the magic effect of presence" Kataev is clearly greatly indebted to Mandelshtam, whom he calls "The Exile," and quotes as saying: "Is the thing really the master of the word? The word is a psyche. A living word does not denote an object, it freely chooses, as if for its dwelling, this or that objective sense, substantiveness, pleasant body. And the word wanders freely around the thing, like a soul around a body from which it has departed but which it has not forgotten" (IX, 494).[49]

As an example of a psyche in Mandelshtam's sense Kataev invents the word *brambakher*, and permits it to assume various meanings in accordance with Mandelshtam's view that an object is not master of a word. *Brambakher* pursues Kataev (and his characters, Monsieur and Madame) throughout East Germany. The word is derived from the name of a small German spa, Bad Brambach, and one of its applications is to the mineral water from this town. But, as a psyche, the word is not limited to this one meaning, and Kataev employs it as a sound threatening war, as the crunch of a wasp's body being crushed underfoot, and the crash of Luther's inkwell on the wall as he struggles against the Devil. Later it is used to express an idea similar to a notion in *The Holy Well*, namely, that the author "becomes" the various objects he is looking at.

When a poet's psyche-word settles in a body (i.e., when a poet describes something), the result is a metaphor; in a few outstanding cases through the "effect of presence," the metaphor will be so striking as to appear to be realized or materialized (this notion is essentially an extension of the idea of stereoscopic description advanced in *The Grass of Oblivion*). It is precisely the magic "effect of presence" which Kataev sees as "the secret essence of truly modern poetry" (IX, 500). In the future, poets may be enabled to achieve even more astounding materialization because of scientific advances. Kataev quotes from a *Pravda* report about information-carrying lasers and holography and predicts that they will one day be used to materialize the artist's images in the reader's room.

However, it is not necessary to await these scientific advances before experiencing the "effect of presence." Examples may be found in modern poetry and elsewhere. As a good example of a metaphor realized as a legend, Kataev cites the well-known story of Luther's throwing an inkwell at the Devil. Mandelshtam claimed that Luther was a poor philologist because he chose to throw an inkwell rather than a word (IX, 498).[50] But, in fact, Luther never threw an inkwell. He struggled with the Devil by writing articles, and in that sense an inkwell was his weapon. "This was immediately turned into a legend which went around the whole world," Kataev adds. "Thus a pun became a metaphor, and the metaphor, in its turn, was all but realized into a historical event, a theatrical scene with the Devil as a participant, something very like the 'effect of presence' " (IX, 498).[51]

B. *The Wasp and the Poodle*

Kataev gives two further examples of the realization of metaphor, in episodes involving a wasp and a poodle. The former is a self-contained two-page description of a man's fight with a wasp. On one level it is a brilliantly realistic piece of descriptive writing which captures the menace of the wasp and the fear of the man. But, like many of the images in this and the preceding works, the wasp is both realistic and symbolic. A clue to the wasp's possible significance lies in a dream which the narrator has in the middle of the section. It is his recurrent dream about Stalin, who is not named, but is described simply as "the man with the narrow eyes of a murderer." Suddenly the narrator is wakened from his dream when the wasp attempts to get into his ear. He jumps up, seizes the wasp, and kills it. The sound of its body being crushed underfoot is described as "a unique sound which seemed to contain all—the chin, the dyed moustache, the crimson turkey skin of his neck, pinched by the standing collar of his emperor's uniform—and the rustle of the dark poison entering my bloodstream and causing my hand to swell up instantly" (IX, 498).

The dream about the narrow-eyed murderer makes it seem reasonable that the man who is suddenly, and apparently inexplicably, conjured up by the sound of the wasp's body being crushed is Stalin, and that the struggle with the wasp represents yet another attempt by Kataev (following those in *The Holy Well*) to exorcise the spirit of Stalinism.

The principal character of the latter part of the tale, the poodle Kubik, comes into being as the result of a similar process of metaphor realization. The poodle in Goethe's *Faust* serves as a model, and when the narrator sees a man and a black poodle in a Weimar street he muses that they might be realizations of Goethe's poetic thought. In a passage recalling the talking cat episode from *The Holy Well*, Kataev claims that his knowledge of poodles derives from the fact that he was once a spoilt little dog himself, although only for a short time. Kataev's description of his time as a poodle (IX, 506–8) may be read as an Aesopian account of the way in which writers became subservient to authority. Thus, the poodle begins as a metaphor for the position of the writer in the Stalin era, but such is the power of poetic thought (to use Kataev's phrase) that he becomes realized as a character—an artificial dog created by an experimental cyberneticist—and takes part in the story with which the work ends.

C. *Why* Kubik?

Near the beginning of *Kubik* the author teasingly raises the question of his work's title. The word *kubik* means a little cube or block, and Kataev writes: "But why, in fact, *kubik*? Because it is six sides in three dimensions of time and space. Or perhaps it is simply the name of a dog. Or, most likely, for no reason. I simply wanted it that way. What can be better than one's free will!" (IX, 463)

The link between a cube ("six sides in three dimensions") and a dog is not evident at this juncture, but once the dog is introduced and described as "an artificial creation in time and space" (IX, 511), the reason for the choice of name begins to emerge. The dog is an example of "the magic effect of presence"—a three-dimensional figure created through the artist's power of poetic thought. All the references to cubes in the work—including the name of the dog—have to do with the artist's ability to depict the material world with great clarity and solidity. They thus point to the theme of artistic, and particularly poetic, creativity as the central one in the work. For example, the ability of the artist to immortalize something in his work is expressed in terms of the flash-cube used in a camera. Or again, the article on holography includes the following words: "One cubic centimeter of matter possessing the effect of three-dimensional photography (holography) . . . can contain as much information as five million books" (IX, 499). It may appear that such technical advances will render poets unnecessary, and that, therefore, the *Pravda* report runs counter to the defense of poetry Kataev undertakes in *Kubik*. However, by emphasizing the power of poets like Mandelshtam to create "the effect of presence," Kataev indicates that true artists have nothing to fear from holography's "cubic centimeter." The future achievement of information-science is no more astounding than the present achievement of the best modern poets. Thus, the various references to cubes pertain to the nature of artistic creativity, and a work which at first appears to have no unifying theme can be seen to be about art, and particularly poetry. *Kubik* is essentially a tone poem about the nature of poetry.

Concerned as it is almost exclusively with aesthetic matters, *Kubik* demonstrates why Kataev was attracted all his life by such an aesthete as Bunin. It is fitting that his work of the 1960s—in which he constantly scrutinizes the place of pure artistry within the framework of Soviet society—should end with *Kubik*, for the publication of that tale indicates that aestheticism is now tolerated, although the critical response to all of Kataev's works of this period demonstrates that his approach to art is certainly not universally accepted.[52]

VI *Works of the 1970s*

Thus far three out of Kataev's four works of the 1970s have continued the pattern set by *The Holy Well* and *The Grass of Oblivion*. With the exception of "Violet," the works of the 1970s have all had an inward focus. They are structured through associative links in the author's mind and deal with his own past or his former friends or his family history refracted through the "magic crystal" of his memory, so that what emerges is not historical truth, but his own version of events.[53] It is now clear that Kataev takes the notion of *mauvisme* seriously, for he persists in using the term to describe his current style of writing more than ten years after he introduced it in *The Holy Well*. The major features of *mauvisme*—the rejection of chronology as the natural structural principle in artistic prose and the emphasis on spontaneity—are as prominent in *A Mosaic of Life*, *The Cemetery at Skulyany*, and *My Diamond Crown* as in the works of the 1960s.

A. A Mosaic of Life

The influence of Olesha's *Not a Day Without a Line* on *The Holy Well* and *The Grass of Oblivion* has already been noted. Kataev's memoirs of childhood, *A Mosaic of Life* (1972), exhibit that influence even more clearly. Olesha's work is a collection of short, self-contained passages, ranging in length from a few lines to two or three pages, on a variety of autobiographical topics. Its fragmentary nature may well stem from Olesha's severe creative difficulties, but he justifies it by arguing that in the modern world readers require books consisting of short passages which may be read in the odd free moments of a busy life.[54] Kataev's memoirs (he himself rejects the term, but it is nevertheless applicable to *A Mosaic of Life*) likewise consist of short passages—over one hundred of them—each of which deals with an aspect of the author's childhood. The literal translation of the work's title is *A Fragmented Life*, and in a letter to his granddaughter which, characteristically, forms not the first but the fifth section, Kataev comments on the disjointed nature of the work by quoting from Tolstoy's diary of 1904: "If I have time and strength in the evenings then I must write down my recollections without ordering them, just as they come. I've started remembering so vividly."[55]

Like Olesha, Kataev strives to recapture the physical experience of his childhood. Olesha's words, "these notes are an attempt to restore my life . . . sensually,"[56] also apply to Kataev's vivid recollections of his childhood. Kataev's awareness of two distinct personas, his boyhood self and himself now, and his attempts to distinguish between the perception of these two figures, as he had in earlier works through the figure of Ryurik Pchelkin, recall Olesha's distinction between "the boy" and "the author" in *Not a Day Without a Line*.[57] Finally, there are several textual similarities between Olesha's work and Kataev's which may be explained by the authors' similar childhood experiences. Both works mention notable Odessa characters such as Sergey Utochkin; in both there is a memorable picture of the early days of soccer in Odessa; and both display a fascination with technological achievements, particularly with "the miracle of manned flight."

Many of Kataev's earlier works had been based in part on his recollections of childhood, so that it is no surprise to find in *A Mosaic of Life* echoes of incidents described in "Yuletide at Pokoy," "Rodion Zhukov," *Lone White Sail, The Electric Machine,* and other works. A passage in *A Mosaic of Life* entitled "The Theater" repeats the story, first told in "Yuletide at Pokoy," of Kataev's early attempts at amateur dramatics. "The Hydrogen Explosion" and "Another Explosion" delineate a fascination with the magic effects of scientific experiments which clearly inspired the tale *The Electric Machine.* Several passages deal with visits to Akkerman and journeys on the Black Sea steamers featured in such fictional works as "Rodion Zhukov" and *Lone White Sail.* The poignancy of first love, explored in fictionalized form in *The Small Farm in the Steppe,* and—more personally—in *The Holy Well,* recurs in the penultimate passage in *A Mosaic of Life.* Here again, Kataev claims that the love he first experienced as a boy would last throughout his life. On the other hand, in *My Diamond Crown* Kataev returns to the theme of unrequited love, which he sees as the greatest spur to artistic creativity, although the love affair that he recalls in that work is the passionate one with Bulgakov's sister which inspired the autobiographical story of 1923, "In Winter." Thus it would be erroneous to see in a particular adolescent love affair the source of the recurrent theme of unrequited love in Kataev's work. The sense of separation and loss engendered by that theme may have its roots in real incidents from Kataev's life, but it is always poetically transformed so that it transcends particular experiences. Finally, the theme of money, important in many earlier works, recurs time and time again in the pages of *A Mosaic of Life.* As Kataev says: "Oh, money, money! How many times have I had occasion to mention money in this book. But what can you do about it? That's life."[58] The impulsive and reckless young hero's fantastic schemes—such as catching spar-

rows by making them drunk, or buying a punt and sailing out to
sea in it, or producing hydrogen at home—all require money, and
he goes to extraordinary lengths to obtain it. Thus, *A Mosaic of Life*
demonstrates the importance of autobiographical elements in Kataev's work by drawing together the network of recurrent detail in
much of his earlier writing. Its chief charm, however, lies in its
evocation of an Odessan childhood in the first years of this century.

B. *"Violet"*

Of all Kataev's works written since 1964, "Violet" is the only one
in which he does not refer directly to himself. Yet this story (turned
into a play by Kataev and successfully produced on television) is
not so much of an exception in the context of his later works as it
appears at first sight. The action of the story takes place in a retirement home for senior Party officials. The oldest and most re-
spected inmate—Ekaterina Gerasimovna Novoselova, whose
underground nickname was "Violet"—is visited by her former husband who wishes to see her again before his imminent death. Many
years earlier she had helped him through college and nominated
him for Party membership. Then, when he had begun his career
as a Stalinist administrator, he became infatuated with a younger
woman, denounced his wife to the secret police, and married the
beautiful but heartless social climber. Now, mortally ill, he comes
to ask his first wife's forgiveness. She meets him but cannot forgive
him, and after his death refuses to attend his funeral.

Although Ekaterina Gerasimovna can clearly not be identified
with the author, her fate echoes a recurrent theme in Kataev's
autobiographical work: the reward in old age for keeping faith with
the Revolution.[59] The emigré widow in *The Holy Well* suffers terrible loneliness, whereas the narrator has his beloved homeland,
which he describes as much like the land around the old people's
home in "Violet," set in Kataev's home village of Peredelkino.[60]
Similarly, in *The Grass of Oblivion* Bunin is portrayed as a lonely,
poverty-stricken old man without a homeland.

But emigration is not the only way of turning one's back on the
Revolution, and "Violet" has wider implications than similar situations in previous works. In the figure of his heroine Kataev em-
bodies the idealistic side of the Revolution before its temporary
slide into terror under Stalin. Similarly, Novoselov represents the

darker side of the Revolution: he applauds Ivan the Terrible's use
of violence to impose his will. Now, in the ultimate fate of the two
characters, virtue is rewarded and cowardice and selfishness pun-
ished. Yet the story's symbolism—its commentary on the path of
the Revolution—is complicated by the fact that Ekaterina Gerasimovna is partly responsible for her husband's rise to power. After
all, she helped him gain his position. Moreover, there is a hint that
one of the minor characters, another inmate of the home, may have
been the judge who sentenced Ekaterina Gerasimovna. If this is so,
then at least some of those who perverted the Revolution are still
honored by the Party. The questions about the Revolution and the
links between past and present raised by "Violet" are not, therefore,
so glibly answered as they may appear to be.

It is significant that in his only nonpersonal work of recent years
Kataev should restate one of the basic problems of *The Holy Well*
and *The Grass of Oblivion:* the question of the course of the Revolution and the link between one's present position and past actions.

CHAPTER 7

Conclusion

THE development of Kataev's long and diverse career has followed major trends in Soviet literature. During the 1920s he
was a gifted but typical fellow-traveler, working with facility in a
number of genres and making no strong political points. His humor,
sharp observation of everyday life, and interest in distorted perception make this period his richest (although some of his recent
works have also been very good). In the 1930s he followed the path
taken by most of the former fellow-travelers, turning out works of
Socialist Realism: *Time, Forward!*, one of the best examples of the
"construction novels" of the first Five Year Plan era, and *Lone White
Sail*, one of the most notable Soviet novels for children. During and
after World War II Kataev continued to produce topical works, but
of much lower quality. He played an indirect but important part
in the Thaw as editor of *Yunost*. In the 1960s, too, his work has
contributed to important trends in Soviet literature. Freed from
the constraints of the previous age, many older writers turned then
to memoirs of the repressive days of the recent past; a greater
awareness of the rest of the world penetrated Soviet literature;
authors began to experiment more with form and to reveal a more
sophisticated taste in the arts than before. Kataev's works of the
1960s reflect all of these innovations.

Thus, perhaps the most obvious point to be made about Kataev
is that he has almost always been in tune with the age. Yet, diverse
as his career has been, certain constant factors give his work its
individuality and link early and late periods. Let us consider Kataev's weaknesses before going on to his strengths.

Kataev is the author of many plays, but by his own admission is
"an indifferent dramatist."[1] He has recently said: "My serious plays
were unsuccessful. My thought can be transmitted only in prose."[2]

In quantitative terms, the tetralogy *Black Sea Waves* is Kataev's
major work, yet apart from *Lone White Sail* it is an artistic failure

145

for reasons that cast much light on the nature of his talent. First, he lacks the ability to sustain the characterization of adults. In an extended narrative his imagined characters turn out flat and stereotyped, with the exception of those based on himself and, to a lesser extent, his father. In other words, he lacks the imagination to people his novels with believable characters.

Similarly—again with one or two notable exceptions—Kataev cannot depict with complexity the society in which his novels are set. His works focus backward to his own past and inward rather than toward the social world around him. The best pages of all four novels of the tetralogy deal with the hero's purely private concerns, and especially with his sensuous perception of the physical world. When placing these private concerns in their wider social setting of war and revolution, Kataev falters.

It must be concluded, then, that Kataev's gifts are not primarily those of the novelist, and his achievement in the field of the novel proper is inferior to, say, Leonid Leonov's. His best periods have been those in which he has not attempted the conventional novel: the 1920s, the 1960s, and the 1970s. Paradoxically, however, three of his finest works—*The Embezzlers*, *Time, Forward!*, and *Lone White Sail*—are novels, but their peculiarity lies in the fact that in each of them Kataev's weakness in adult characterization matters little. The two embezzlers are deliberately portrayed superficially, in a Gogolian manner. *Time, Forward!* is not vitiated by its superficial characters, for its pace, atmosphere, and cinematic technique make it a stylized evocation of a particular time, in which the rows of opposing one-sided characters are appropriate. In the case of *Lone. White Sail* the adults merely form a background for the adventures of children, with whom Kataev can identify, and whom he portrays vividly. In similar fashion, his successful works of recent years have rarely contained invented adult characters.

To a considerable degree, Kataev's strengths are those of the lyric poet transposed into prose. He writes more convincingly of emotions and physical sensations than of ideas, and he has few rivals among prose writers in the depiction of material objects. His recall of sense impressions and his ability to convey them through comparisons is one of his outstanding strengths. His very well developed sense of humor added to this explains how he recreates with such authenticity the atmosphere of his childhood.

Kataev's work poses few contemporary moral dilemmas. The one serious choice which dominates his later work occurred in the past: the decision to remain in Russia and adapt to changing circumstances. Russia emerges as one of the most important of Kataev's values; the other is culture, particularly Russian poetry. Everything else stands noticeably lower in his hierarchy of values. Precisely his aestheticism, over the past decade or so, has alienated certain critics, who have, with some justification, gained the impression that nothing is safe from Kataev's eye, that there is nothing and no one so precious to him that he will refuse to step back and describe it with cold accuracy.

Yet although essentially an aesthete, Kataev is not content to remain a private writer, a lyricist pure and simple. Herein lies the key to his duality. In *The Grass of Oblivion* he reveals the profundity of the split within himself between the aesthete and the Soviet writer committed to supporting the regime in his works.

It is interesting to speculate, as Nadezhda Mandelshtam has, on what might have become of this "very talented man, with a lively intelligence and a quick wit, who belongs to the most enlightened wing of the present-day best-selling Soviet writers"[3] if he had not been obliged to adapt to the demands of Socialist Realism. Yet to speculate in this way is, of course, fruitless, because Kataev is as temperamentally incapable of shaking off his "public" side as of discarding his "private" side. His inherent aestheticism has been checked and modified by a need to publish and achieve public recognition and—in recent years at any rate—by a deep commitment to his country and its political system.

Kataev's position in Soviet literature is a secure one. If he stands a little below the first rank of Soviet authors (a conclusion that he himself seems to reach in *My Diamond Crown*, where he compares himself unfavorably with such "classics" as Bulgakov and Olesha),[4] he occupies an important place in the next rank as the author of some enduring works, as a representative of several distinct phases of Soviet literature, and as one of the foremost masters of the Russian language of the past sixty years.

Notes and References

Chapter One

1. See V. Kataev, "Avtobiografiia," in V. Lidin (ed.), *Pisateli: avtobiografii sovremennikov* (Moscow, 1928), pp. 175–77. Cited below as: "Avtobiografiia" (1928).

2. In a letter to Bunin of August 13, 1914, Kataev writes that he will shortly be leaving Odessa for the "theater of war." See *Literaturnoe nasledstvo*, vol. 84, *Ivan Bunin* (Book 2) (Moscow, 1973), p. 461.

3. Kataev's early works appeared in *Odesskii vestnik, Odesskii listok, Iuzhnaia mysl'*, and other Odessa newspapers, and in the Petrograd journals *Ves' mir, Probuzhdenie*, and *Lukomor'e*.

4. The atmosphere of Odessa in the Civil War is very well evoked in the diary of Vera Nikolaevna Bunina. See M. Greene (ed.), *Ustami Buninykh (The Bunins Speak)* (Frankfurt/Main, 1977), I, pp. 177–348.

5. On this society see the untitled contribution by B. Bobovich to O. Suok-Olesha and E. Pel'son (eds.), *Vospominaniia o Iurii Oleshe* (Moscow, 1975), pp. 22–26.

6. G. Dolinov, "Vospominaniia ob odesskom literaturno-khudozhestvennom kruzhke 'Zelenaia lampa,'" unpublished manuscript quoted in L. Skorino, *Pisatel' i ego vremia (A Writer and his Time)* (Moscow, 1965), pp. 103–4. Cited below as: Skorino.

7. On this society see L. Slavin, "Moi Olesha," in *Portrety i zapiski* (Moscow, 1965), pp. 10–11.

8. *Ustami Buninykh*, pp. 180, 188.

9. V. Kataev, "Avtobiografiia," in B. Brainina and E. Nikitina (eds.), *Sovetskie pisateli. Avtobiografii* (Moscow, 1959), 1, pp. 538–40. Cited below as: "Avtobiografiia" (1959).

10. "Avtobiografiia" (1928), p. 176.

11. Vera Nikolaevna writes: "If Kataev comes I'll give him a piece of my mind which he won't forget. After all, is it so long ago that he was strutting around in Volunteer's epaulettes?" *Ustami Buninykh*, p. 241.

12. "Avtobiografiia" (1959). The modern equivalent of ROSTA is TASS. The "satire windows" refer to the fact that, in view of the shortage of paper,

149

the windows of newspaper offices were used to display satirical posters, etc. "Oral newspapers," designed to overcome the same difficulty, consisted of live performances at factories and offices by journalists who read the news and satirical sketches.

13. For straightforward accounts of the incident see Kataev's article "Spasibo za eto gazete," *Literaturnaia gazeta*, May 5, 1933; and his "Avtobiografiia" (1959).

14. See the autobiographical stories "Chernyi khleb" ("Black Bread"), I, 428–35; and "Krasivye shtany" ("Fine Trousers"), II, 24–31.

15. N. Mandelstam, *Hope against Hope* (London, 1971), p. 279. Cited below as: N. Mandelstam.

16. Something of the atmosphere of a Moscow into which young authors were pouring daily can be gained from Kataev's story "Fantomy" ("Phantoms"), II, 70–83.

17. I. Kremlev, *V literaturnom stroiu* (Moscow, 1968), p. 203. The pamphlet mentioned is Kataev's "O novoi zhilishchnoi politike" (Moscow, 1922). Cited below as: Kremlev.

18. See L. Kroichik, "O nekotorykh zakonomernostiakh razvitiia sovetskogo fel'etona," in *Revoliutsiia, zhizn', pisatel'* (Voronezh, 1969), pp. 73–88.

19. See A. Erlikh, "Oni rabotali v gazete," *Znamia*, 1958, no. 8, p. 170. Cited below as: Erlikh.

20. Kataev has recently recounted several stories about events in his apartment on Mylnikov Lane in *Almaznyi moi venets (My Diamond Crown)*, *Novyi mir*, 1978, no. 6, pp. 3–146.

21. For an account of the latter occasion, which took place in 1921, see Iu. Olesha, *Ni dnia bez strochki (Not a Day Without a Line)* (Moscow, 1965), p. 144.

22. Erlikh, p. 180.

23. See *The Grass of Oblivion*; also R. Pospelov, "Beseda s V. Kataevym," *Literatura i zhizn'*, January 31, 1962. Cited below as: Pospelov.

24. Skorino, p. 197. Gorky called *The Embezzlers* "a work of great talent": M. Gor'kii, *Sobranie sochinenii* (Moscow, 1949–55), XXX, p. 6.

25. See F. Mikhal'skii and M. Rogachevskii (eds.), *Moskovskii Khudozhestvennyi teatr v sovetskuiu epokhu* (Moscow, 1974), p. 545.

26. Stanislavsky's words are quoted in N. Gorchakov, "Rabota K. S. Stanislavskogo nad sovetskoi p'esoi," in *Voprosy rezhissury* (Moscow, 1954), p. 103.

27. The 1935 New York production had a spurious anti-Soviet ending. See J. Krutch, "Soviet Farce," *The Nation*, October 23, 1935, p. 490.

28. I. Mashbits-Verov, "Na grani: Tvorchestvo Valentina Kataeva," *Na literaturnom postu*, 1930, no. 9, pp. 35–46; and no. 11, pp. 47–56. Cited below as: Mashbits-Verov.

29. I. Babel', "Rech' na Pervom Vsesoiuznom s"ezde sovetskikh pisatelei," *Izbrannoe* (Moscow, 1966), p. 410. Cited below as: Babel'.

30. See Kataev, "Nepovtorimye, geroicheskie dni," VIII, 298–302.

31. Socialist competition is a scheme whereby two factories or other concerns undertake to compete with each other in productivity.

32. "To, chto ia videl," *Literaturnaia gazeta*, July 1, 1929.

33. G. Aleksandrov, "V. Kataev i P. Pavlenko o sovetskikh rabochikh," *Molodaia gvardiia*, 1929, no. 16, pp. 75–77. See also N. Iakovlev, "Poshliaki na literaturnykh gastroliakh," *Komsomol'skaia pravda*, July 13 , 1929. Kataev was partially defended in an editorial entitled "Ne pomoshch' a pomekha," *Literaturnaia gazeta*, July 22, 1929.

34. "Puteshestvie v stranu budushchego," *30 dnei*, 1929, no. 8, pp. 24–37.

35. The White Sea Canal was built by prisoners, including political prisoners. Solzhenitsyn has written of the "disgraceful book on the White Sea Canal, which was the first in Russian literature to glorify slave labor": *The Gulag Archipelago* (London, 1974), I–II, p. xii.

36. "Pisateli i sotsialisticheskoe stroitel'stvo," *Rost*, 1933, no. 11–12, p. 10.

37. Vera Inber, for example, wrote in her diary that a feeling of inferiority vanished when RAPP was liquidated. See her *Sobranie sochinenii* (Moscow, 1965–6), IV, 426.

38. "Itogi goda," *Vercherniaia Moskva*, April 22, 1933.

39. In 1933 Kataev was quoted as saying: "At the moment I am in a transitional period—a period when I am trying to go beyond the old form, the old artistic devices. And this period has naturally given rise to creative difficulties." V. Sobolev, "Izgnanie metafory," *Literaturnaia gazeta*, May 17, 1933. Cited below as: Sobolev.

40. It was not only writers who produced works for or about children in the mid-1930s. Prokofiev's musical tale *Peter and the Wolf* was composed in 1936, and Deyneka's painting of three boys looking at a flying-boat, *Future Pilots*, dates from 1937. Thus, *Lone White Sail* forms part of a general trend in the arts at this time.

41. See an autobiographical note in V. Lidin (ed.), *Literaturnaia Rossiia: Sbornik sovremennoi prozy* (Moscow, 1924), pp. 147–50.

42. N. Mandelstam, p. 277.

43. "Avtobiografiia" (1959).

44. See Erlikh, pp. 188–89, for an account of Kataev's reaction to the news of Petrov's death, which reached him when he was staying in the Hotel Moskva in Moscow.

45. "Avtobiografiia" (1959).

46. See V. Pomerantsev, "Ob iskrennosti v literature," *Novyi mir*, 1953, no. 12, pp. 218–45.

47. Aksenov defended *The Holy Well* from the severe censure of the critic and novelist Dudintsev. See the former's article "Puteshestvie k Kataevu," *Iunost'*, 1967, no. 1, pp. 68–69.

48. Kataev mentions these lecture tours in *My Diamond Crown*.

49. See Kataev's article "O Gor'kom" (VIII, 371–74). This article is part of his speech at the Second Congress of Soviet Writers in 1954.

50. "Avtobiografiia" (1959).

51. For a discussion of this topic with particular reference to "Fialka" ("Violet," 1973), see V. Iverni, "Sotsrealizm s chelovecheskim litsom," *Kontinent*, 1976, no. 7, pp. 393–417.

Chapter Two

1. Kataev's early poems, which include such titles as "V khrame" and "K Tebe, Khristos," were published in Odessa newspapers from 1910 onward.

2. See *The Grass of Oblivion*, IX, 263–64.

3. "Sukhovei," IX, 545; "Znoi," IX, 548; "Kassiopeia," IX, 562.

4. "Spring Chimes," I, 51–64; "The Gun," I, 65–71. "Yuletide at Pokoy" was published in *Ves' mir* (Petrograd), 1918, no. 7, pp. 2–9.

5. For these sketches see Kataev's *Pochti dnevnik* (Moscow, 1962).

6. See, for example, "1915 god," *Odesskii listok*, January 5, 1915; "Rus', Stansy o voine," *Ves' mir*, 1915, no. 1, p. 21.

7. For a discussion of "At Night" see Skorino, p. 92.

8. See VIII, 7–39.

9. Both stories were written in Odessa (in 1919 and 1920 respectively), but published only after Kataev moved to Moscow. The same was true of other stories of the period.

10. Like Germann, Krants has a German surname and values self-control, precision, and reason while at the same time harboring unrecognized destructive passions. The opening sentence of Chapter 3 echoes the opening of Pushkin's story.

11. See Skorino, pp. 172–73; and T. Sidel'nikova, *Valentin Kataev: ocherk zhizni i tvorchestva* (Moscow, 1957), pp. 32–33. Cited below as: Sidel'nikova.

12. The closing words of this passage recur with slight modifications in other stories of this period.

13. In a slightly self-congratulatory passage from *The Grass of Oblivion* Kataev recalls: "And we, those same young ones at whom [Bunin] banged his stick were Bagritsky, Olesha, and I. At that time people in town used to say of us with a mixture of terror and astonishment: 'Oh, those three . . . .'" (IX, 327)

14. Originally conceived as part of a longer work to be called *Pokhozhdeniia trekh bezdel'nikov*—a loosely structured narrative about three dreamers with an enthusiasm for the Revolution. Similar characters were portrayed by Kataev in his film scenario *Poet* (*The Poet*, 1957) (IV, 429–86).

15. The phrase "made strange" is a commonly accepted English version of the term *ostranenie*.

16. Kataev links "Sir Henry and the Devil" with *The Holy Well* in an interview entitled "Obnovlenie prozy," *Voprosy literatury*, 1971, no. 2, pp. 23–31.

17. It lay unpublished for a further three years, probably because the censor held it up. Kataev writes: "The first number of *Krasnaya nov* contains my favorite story 'The Father,' which 'for reasons beyond the control of the journal's management' has lain in the desk for three years." "Pisateli o sebe," *Na literaturnom postu*, 1928, no. 6, p. 91.

18. V. Rossolovskaia, "Tvorchestvo Valentina Kataeva," *Molodaia gvardiia*, 1933, no. 6, pp. 125–32. Cited below as: Rossolovskaia.

19. See, for example, B. Brainina, "O nekotorykh osobennostiakh stilia V. Kataeva," in *Sovetskaia khudozhestvennaia proza: sbornik statei* (Moscow, 1955), pp. 360–94, especially pp. 383–86.

20. V. Sizykh, "Nekotorye osobennosti masterstva V. Kataeva," *Uchenye zapiski Ussuriiskogo gos. ped. instituta*, 1958, no. 2, pp. 217–39.

21. "In Winter" and "Eduard the Loafer" were to have formed part of *Pokhozhdeniia trekh bezdel'nikov*.

22. There can be no doubt that "In Winter" is largely autobiographical. One of Kataev's lyric poems deals with the same subject. See "Kiev" (IX, 603). In a conversation with the present author in 1976 Kataev revealed that the girl with whom he had fallen in love in the early 1920s was Bulgakov's sister. Confirmation of this comes in *My Diamond Crown*, where several of the incidents and key phrases of "In Winter" are repeated.

23. *About That* (sometimes translated as *It*) appeared in the first issue of *LEF* (March 1923). It is significant that in a work where Kataev's commitment to the romantic aspect of the Revolution is made clear the most important influence should be Mayakovsky's.

24. The distortion of perception is quite a common subject in Soviet literature of the 1920s.

25. Only the hero of the very early story "Probuzhdenie" ("The Awakening," 1912) belongs to an older generation. Like Zhukov, he participates in the revolution of 1905.

26. See Skorino, p. 267; B. Brainina, *Valentin Kataev: ocherk tvorchestva* (Moscow, 1960), p. 29.

27. See the note about the story on I, 600.

Chapter Three

1. P. Henry, *Classics of Soviet Satire* (London, 1972), p. vii.

2. See, for example, A. Vulis, *Sovetskii satiricheskii roman* (Tashkent, 1965). Cited below as: Vulis; L. Ershov, *Sovetskaia satiricheskaia proza* (Moscow-Leningrad, 1966).

3. B. G. Guerney calls Kataev "primarily a satirist and humorist," in *Russian Literature in the Soviet Period from Gorki to Pasternak* (New York,

1960), p. 55. E. J. Brown has written: "Valentin Katayev (1897–) might very well be treated as a satirist." See his *Russian Literature since the Revolution* (New York, 1963), p. 133.

4. Several of the details in "The Gold Nib" are repeated in the account of Bunin's final days in Odessa contained in *The Grass of Oblivion*, as, for example, the story of his narrow escape from the Cheka. Vera Bunina reveals in her diary that Bunin did indeed publish a dangerous article on the eve of the Bolshevik entry into Odessa in April 1919 (*Ustami Buninykh*, p. 221).

5. It is so regarded by at least one Soviet critic. See B. Sarnov, "Ugl' pylaiushchii i kimval briatsaiushchii," *Voprosy literatury*, 1968, no. 1, pp. 21–49. Cited below as: Sarnov. In the section on *The Grass of Oblivion* in the present book the argument will be advanced that Kataev may well have come to look on "The Gold Nib" as a justifiable betrayal.

6. "The Pregnant Man" and all other stories and sketches discussed in this section may be found in *Sobranie sochinenii*, vol. II.

7. Kataev continued to write the occasional "verbal cartoon" of this type throughout the 1930s and into the 1940s. See especially his wartime sketches "Kraski Gebbel'sa" (II, 456–58) and "Razgrommel'" (II, 467–69).

8. See A. Britikov, "Detektivnaia povest' v kontekste prikliuchencheskikh zhanrov," in V. Kovalev (ed.), *Russkaia sovetskaia povest' 20–30kh godov* (Leningrad, 1976), pp. 408–53. Cited below as: Kovalev.

9. See, for example, Ia. Okunev's novel *Griadushchii mir (Future World)* (Petrograd, 1923), in which a scientist discovers the secret of anabiosis and uses it to preserve the life of his daughter and a young man. When they awaken from their state of suspended animation it is to a world in which socialist ideals have been put into practice. In the same author's *Zavtrashnii den' (Tomorrow)* (Moscow, 1924), all the great capitalists are overthrown in a worldwide revolution.

10. *Erendorf Island* was written to attract readers to a provincial newspaper. See Kataev's comment on II, 618.

11. This was a fairly common theme at the time. See also Zamyatin's *Ostrovitiane*.

12. I. Erenburg, *Liudi, gody, zhizn'* (Moscow, 1961), p. 538.

13. V. Kataev, *Povelitel' zheleza* (Velikii Ustiug, 1925), p. 8.

14. Ibid., p. 31.

15. Vulis, p. 149.

16. The literal translation of the title is "knives," but the knives referred to are the targets in a "Toss-the-Hoop" stall.

17. In addition to Kataev's work, see V. Lidin, *Rastrata Glotova, Krasnaia nov'*, 1926, no. 7; and L. Grabar', *Lakhudrin pereulok*, in *Zhuravli i kartech'* (Moscow-Leningrad, 1928). A few months before writing *The Embezzlers* Kataev tackled the same theme in a sketch called "Mrachnyi sluchai" ("A Dreary Incident") which bears a certain resemblance to the longer work (II, 123–26).

18. A colleague recalls that there was a cashier at *Gudok* whom everyone called simply Vanechka. See Kremlev, pp. 199–200.

19. From a conversation with Kataev in Skorino, p. 187. The phrase quoted by Kataev was a common slogan during the Civil War.

20. See, for example, Vulis, p. 185; L. Ershov, "Satiriko-iumoristicheskaia povest'," in Kovalev, pp. 359–60. For the opposite view see V. Ermilov, "Traditsiia i novatorstvo," *Krasnaia nov'* 1940, no. 2, p. 192.

21. Ilf and Petrov's first novel, *Dvenadtsat' stul'ev (The Twelve Chairs)*, was directly inspired by Kataev, to whom it is dedicated. One chapter of *The Twelve Chairs*, omitted from the final version of the novel, parodied Kataev's work. See Vulis, p. 183.

22. The pettiness of his absurd aspiration is emphasized by the detail of his papier-maché horse.

23. This is an example of *ostranenie* ("making it strange"), a very common device in Soviet literature of this period.

24. This is an important feature of Soviet literature of the 1920s and, as Nilsson has shown, it may be found also in the work of certain French authors, notably Jean Giraudoux. See N. A. Nilsson, "Through the Wrong End of Binoculars: An Introduction to Jurij Oleša," *Scando-Slavica*, XI (1965): 40–68. A major difference between Kataev's use of unusual angles of vision and that of, say, Olesha is that in Kataev's work of the 1920s such features always result from a state of temporary derangement caused by drink, drugs, illness, etc., whereas for Olesha they form the uniqueness of the artist's vision. (Although in his short story "Love" Olesha approximates Kataev's manner, in that the unusual vision results from temporary insanity caused by love.)

25. Sidel'nikova, p. 63.

26. V. Shklovskii, "Siuzhet i obraz," *Literaturnaia gazeta*, August 17, 1932.

27. See N. Gorchakov, "Rezhisserskie kommentarii k p'ese V. Kataeva *Kvadratura kruga*," in V. Kataev, *Kvadratura kruga* (Moscow-Leningrad, 1929), pp. 51–56.

28. Kataev originally conceived the idea for *Squaring the Circle* after reading an article in *Komsomol'skaia pravda*. On the theme of sexual morality in literature of the second half of the 1920s see V. Buznik, "Povest' 20kh godov," in Kovalev, pp. 204–6.

29. V. Golubov, "Kuda vedet *Doroga tsvetov?*," *Sovetskoe iskusstvo*, May 17, 1934.

30. See Ershov, "Satiriko-iumoristicheskaia povest'," in Kovalev, p. 387.

31. V. Krasil'nikov, Review of *Bezdel'nik Eduard, Pechat' i revoliutsiia*, 1925, no. 5–6, pp. 521–2.

32. See the following reviews of *The Embezzlers*: N. Smirnov, *Novyi mir*, 1927, no. 9, pp. 218–19; M. Maizel', *Zvezda*, 1927, no. 6, pp. 156–57; V. Ermilov, *Pravda*, April 29, 1927; A. Shafir, *Krasnaia nov'*, 1927, no. 6, pp. 262–63.

33. A Lezhnev, "*Rastratchiki,*" *Pechat' i revoliutsiia,* 1927, no. 4, pp. 193–94.

34. See Rossolovskaia, pp. 125–32.

35. Mashbits-Verov, no. 9, p. 35.

36. Ibid., no. 11, p. 55.

37. This is the significance of the title of Mashbits-Verov's article, which means "On the Brink."

38. For an interesting view of the effect of this enforced transformation on fellow-travelers see A. Gladkov, "Slova, slova, slova . . . ," *Rossiia/Russia: Studi i ricerche a cura di Vittorio Strada* (Turin), 1 (1974), pp. 185–240.

Chapter Four

1. N. Mandelstam, p. 279.

2. Ibid., p. 278.

3. See "Entuziazm - planovost' - pobeda," *Magnitorgorskii rabochii,* May 31, 1931. For an account of the background to the novel see Skorino, pp. 225–39.

4. The quoted phrase comes from "To, chto ia videl." It is worth pointing out that in 1930 productivity at Magnitogorsk had been very low, which led to the introduction of socialist competition among brigades in an attempt to improve matters.

5. See *The Grass of Oblivion,* IX, 411–12.

6. At least part of Fenya's journey must be a flashback, but it is made to appear part of the events of the day.

7. "Pisateli na Magnitostroe. Beseda s A. Malyshkinym i V. Kataevym," *Literaturnaia gazeta,* March 11, 1932.

8. I. Anisimov, "Kniga o pafose novogo stroitel'stva," *Literaturnaia gazeta,* February 5, 1933.

9. "Moskva etim letom," *30 dnei,* 1930, no. 9, pp. 56–65.

10. Ibid. and III, 196. By slowing down the dive, rather as a slow-motion camera would, Kataev seems to turn a fall into a flight. This is in keeping with the theme of the novel; man's grace and technique enable him to overcome nature.

11. "Rovesniki kino," VIII, 314.

12. Ibid. Among the many authors influenced by the cinema was the American John Dos Passos, whose work was well known in the Soviet Union and may have provided a model for *Time, Forward!*

13. See III, 139 and 423. Stalin's speech was delivered on February 4, 1931 and printed in *Pravda* the following day. See J. V. Stalin, "The Tasks of Business Executives," *Works* (Moscow, 1955), XIII, pp. 31–44.

14. Russian authors showed a great interest in America in the 1920s and early 1930s. Their attitude was frequently a mixture of admiration for its

technological achievements and censure of its social system. See, for example, some of Mayakovsky's poems about America.

15. "Raport semnadtsatomu," *Literaturnaia gazeta*, December 29, 1933.

16. In his essay "Porogi" Kataev makes the point that in the early 1930s normal prose style seemed old-fashioned and too leisurely to suit the age: "Epoch and style have parted company. The old forms no longer correspond to the scale and quality of the new subject-matter" (VIII, 223).

17. One critic has suggested that near the beginning of the novel such lists are composed of singular nouns, i.e., specific objects, whereas later the lists consist largely of plural nouns. This is seen as evidence of the process of shunning particulars in favor of abstraction which was taking place in Soviet literature at this time. See R. A. Maguire, "Literary Conflicts in the 1920's," *Survey*, 1972, no. 1, pp. 124–7. Cited below as: Maguire.

18. From his early poetry onwards Kataev has shown a preference for dynamic nature descriptions, a feature which may be linked with his liking for a traveling hero, as in "Rodion Zhukov" and *The Embezzlers*.

19. Of course, Kataev was not the only Soviet author of the 1920s and early 1930s to show an interest in the relativity of size. Olesha and Kaverin are two among many who shared this interest. The concept of relativity in time and space provoked much discussion in the Russian popular press in the 1920s, when several articles were devoted to Einstein and Bergson.

20. The implied comparison between the Civil War and the rapid industrialization of the first Five Year Plan period is a common one in literature of these years. It is worth noting that Margulies, at the front, seeks aid from the rear (Moscow) before attempting to break the record. He does not act purely on his own initiative (cf. Chernoivanenko in *For the Power of the Soviets*).

21. "Siuzhet i obraz."

22. "Raport semnadtsatomu."

23. "Siuzhet i obraz."

24. See, for example, F. Gladkov, "Moia rabota nad *Energiei*," in *Energiia* (Moscow, 1934), pp. 21–22.

25. Kataev's only published article about Mark Twain appeared in 1950: See "Mark Tven i Amerika," *Novyi mir*, 1950, no. 5, pp. 229–38. In his review of *Lone White Sail* Shklovsky drew attention to the links with *The Adventures of Tom Sawyer*. As had become almost traditional by then in his reviews of Kataev's works, he criticized the unintegrated images, comparing Kataev unfavorably with Twain in this respect. See his "O Marke Tvene i o tom, kto emu blizok," *Detskaia literatura*, 1938, no. 20, pp. 21–27.

26. It is significant that the atmosphere of *Lone White Sail* should closely resemble that of Kataev's memoirs of childhood, *A Mosaic of Life*. It must be said, though, that the author has stressed the fictional nature of *Lone White Sail*. He says of fiction based loosely on personal experience that

"the closer [events] are to the truth, the greater the degree of fiction" (VIII, 412).

27. See Sobolev.

28. See S. Gekht, "*Rasskazy* V. Kataeva," *Literaturnoe obozrenie*, 1937, no. 12, pp. 3–6.

29. V. Pertsov, "Epos i kharakter," *Literaturnaia gazeta*, January 30, 1938.

30. V. Ermilov, "Povest' o narodnom schast'e," *Krasnaia nov'*, 1937, no. 11, pp. 229–42.

31. For a detailed comparison see N. Maliavkina, "Povest' V. Kataeva *Ia, syn trudovogo naroda,*" in *Voprosy literatury (sbornik statei)* (Petrozavodsk, 1960), pp. 3–33.

Chapter Five

1. See M. Hayward, "The Decline of Socialist Realism," *Survey*, 1972, no. 1, p. 87.

2. *Pochti dnevnik*, pp. 222–25. It is interesting to note that in his World War I stories Kataev had also made use of the contrast between peaceful scenes of everyday life and the horrors of war.

3. Ibid., pp. 228–32.

4. Kataev recalls that he wrote *The Wife* in Kuibyshev, which he had to visit in connection with his brother's death. See the notes to the tale, IV, 490.

5. B. Brainina, "Khrustal'naia bukhta," *Znamia*, 1944, no. 4, p. 150.

6. At least one commentator has cast doubt on the veracity of Kataev's account of life in the catacombs. Alexander Werth, who also visited Odessa after its liberation and spoke to the same partisan leaders as Kataev, reaches a different conclusion about the importance of their role. See his *Russia at War* (London, 1964), pp. 823–24.

7. Kataev at first intended to call his novel *The Pioneers* (the name of a Soviet youth organization). See *Vecherniaia Moskva*, January 1, 1946. Extracts from the novel were published as booklets for children, and the completed novel was published simultaneously in *Novyi mir* (1949, Nos. 6, 7, 8) and the children's newspaper *Pionerskaia pravda* July 12 - October 21, 1949).

8. M. Bubennov, "O novom romane Valentina Kataeva *Za vlast' Sovetov,*" *Pravda*, January 16, 17, 1950.

9. *Pravda*, January 24, 1950. It should be remembered that at this period Party interest in the orthodoxy of literature was at its highest.

10. See A. Yarmolinsky, *Literature under Communism*, (Bloomington, 1960), p. 55.

11. See "Mysli o tvorchestve," VIII, 417.

12. Ibid., pp. 410–11.

13. For some of the scenes on the farm Kataev drew on a cycle of poems published in *Odesskii listok* in July 1915. One poem from this cycle ("Znoi," *Odesskii listok*, July 21, 1915) is paraphrased and incorporated in its entirety. The details of the walk in the steppe with Marina in Chapter 4 are based on "Noch' trevozhna," *Odesskii listok*, July 17, 1915. The description of Istanbul draws on the poem "Stambul," *Iuzhnaia mysl'*, April 10, 1916.

Chapter Six

1. "Pero zhar-ptitsy," *Literaturnaia gazeta*, May 22, 1959.

2. Kataev "follows" Lenin round Paris, visiting the same places the revolutionary leader had. This method recalls Pushkin's construction of the first chapter of *Evgenii Onegin*.

3. Reflections on the nature of time recur in most of Kataev's subsequent works.

4. The title may refer to H. G. Wells's story "The Door in the Wall," which has as its theme the lost beauty of childhood.

5. "Slovo o novatorstve," *Moskovskii literator*, May 30, 1957. This article was later incorporated into "O novatorstve," VIII, 384–88. The quoted passage is on VIII, 388.

6. "Leninskii dukh novatorstva," *Pravda*, November 10, 1961. Incorporated into "O novatorstve."

7. See Maguire.

8. Of course, detailed descriptions did not entirely disappear in the 1930s and 1940s. *Lone White Sail* is an example of a novel with a good deal of detailed description.

9. "Znat' i verit'," *Literaturnaia gazeta*, December 29, 1955. Incorporated into "Mysli o tvorchestve," VIII, 408–23.

10. "Slovo nado liubit'," *Literaturnaia gazeta*, September 15, 1940. Later in VIII, 335–36.

11. "Novogodnii tost," *Literaturnaia gazeta*, January 1, 1953. Later in VIII, 345–47. The quoted passage is on VIII, 347.

12. Ibid., p. 346. It is interesting to compare this passage with the extract from *The Holy Well* in which Kataev makes a plea for the reintroduction of fantasy into literature (IX, 204).

13. "Ne povtoriat' sebia i drugogo," *Literaturnaia gazeta*, January 1, 1972.

14. Ibid.

15. From a conversation between Kataev and the present author, May 18, 1971. In addition to its reference to *mauvais*, the word *mauvisme* may be coined on the model of *fauvisme*.

16. "Obnovlenie prozy," p. 128.

17. Babel', p. 411.

18. In viewing Kataev's later works in the context of Soviet literature,

as opposed to that of Western literature and film, there is clearly a danger of exaggerating their innovative quality. Nevertheless, as with most works of the Thaw and post-Thaw period, the context deserves consideration. In recent years Kataev has attempted to bring the achievements of modern Western art to the attention of the Soviet public. It is ironic, therefore, and a comment on the pressures exerted on writers in the mid-1930s, that in 1936 he should have published an article condemning the critic D. S. Mirsky for his attempt to popularize James Joyce. See "Vperedi progressa," *Literaturnaia gazeta*, March 10, 1936 (one of a series of articles under the general heading *Protiv formalizma i naturalizma*).

19. Olesha's work appeared posthumously in 1965. In reviewing it Kataev wrote: "Usually the process of the inception and construction of an artistic image takes place in secret, in the depths of the artist's consciousness . . . Olesha brought this process out from the secret recesses of his consciousness for everyone to see, and made it the subject of art, its very content. It would appear no one did this before Olesha. It was his discovery" ("Proshchanie s mirom," VIII, 437).

20. During a conversation with the present author in 1971 Kataev called *mauvisme* a working hypothesis.

21. There are many examples of the theme of prescience in *The Holy Well*, notably where the narrator imagines that he saw the funeral of President Kennedy on television eighteen months before it took place.

22. A. Terts (Sinyavsky's pseudonym), *Fantasticheskii mir Abrama Tertsa* (New York, 1967), p. 446.

23. See "Obnovlenie prozy," p. 131.

24. The spring does exist in Peredelkino, the village near Moscow where Kataev has his home.

25. In most of his later works Kataev uses a first-person narrator who may broadly be equated with himself, inasmuch as his experiences, his family and friends are those of the author. But Kataev is aware that his narrator represents him at different stages of his life, and cannot be unequivocally identified with him as he is now.

26. It is interesting to note that there are traces of Buddhist philosophy in Bunin's work.

27. Nadezhda Mandelshtam paints a similarly grotesque picture of the contrast between her husband's way of life and that of the newly rich (in the 1930s) authors who conformed to the demands of the state. See N. Mandelstam, pp. 227–79.

28. The poem is "Mne Tiflis gorbatyi snilsia," *Sobranie sochinenii* (Washington, 1964), 1, pp. 83–84.

29. *The Holy Well* was, of course, written before the appearance of the Soviet edition of Mandelshtam's poetry (Leningrad, 1973).

30. See a report in *The Times* (London), March 17, 1966, p. 11.

31. In some of his stories Bunin traces a similar relationship between life and art. See, for example, "Solnechnyi udar" ("Sunstroke").

32. One critic has counted some twenty occurrences of the words "scorched" and "burned" describing such things as parts of the body, books, money, etc. See Alayne P. Reilly, *America in Contemporary Soviet Literature* (New York, 1971), p. 134.

33. A similar, heavily sarcastic passage is aimed at the boorishness of Nikita Khrushchev, who had publicly rebuked Kataev for some of his comments to American journalists (IX, 227).

34. V. Rozov, "I ustoiavshimsia ne budet nikogda," *Detskaia literatura*, 1967, no. 1, p. 23.

35. A sense of loss and separation runs through several of Kataev's poems. See especially the poems of 1954 "Rannii sneg" (IX, 643); "U nas dorogi raznye" (IX, 644); and "Bespridannitsa" (IX, 641–42).

36. In a speech delivered on October 19, 1977 Kataev said: "The overwhelming majority of us (still very young writers at the beginning of our careers) chose the Revolution. Do not imagine that this was a very simple or easy choice." *Literaturnaia gazeta*, October 26, 1977.

37. M. Chudakova, *Masterstvo Iuriia Oleshi* (Moscow, 1972), p. 31.

38. The phrase was applied to the Odessan writers by Shklovsky. See "Iugo-zapad," *Literaturnaia gazeta*, January 5, 1933.

39. See Pospelov.

40. While recognizing that much of Kataev's later work cannot be taken as factual, several critics have expressed or implied disappointment at his subjective approach. See, for example, Deming Brown, *Soviet Russian Literature since Stalin* (Cambridge, 1978), p. 256; and A. Subbotin, "Novaia zhizn' Maiakovskogo," *Ural*, 1968, no. 7, pp. 120–27.

41. The passage may be found in Bunin's *Zhizn' Arsen'eva*, *Sobranie sochinenii* (Moscow, 1965–67), VI, p. 235.

42. On this point see E. Ivanova, "Povestvovatel' i avtobiograficheskii geroi v *Trave zabven'ia* V. Kataeva," *Izvestiia Voronezhskogo gos. ped. instituta*, vol. 125 (1972), pp. 142–59. For Kataev's possible debt to Olesha here see pp. 141–42 of the present book.

43. S. Ingulov, "Devushka iz partshkoly," *Kommunist* (Khar'kov), October 2, 1921.

44. This harsh judgement on Bunin was attacked by several Soviet critics. See, for example, Sarnov.

45. See O. Mikhailov, "Put' Bunina-khudozhnika," in *Literaturnoe nasledstvo*, vol. 84, *Ivan Bunin*, Book 1 (Moscow, 1973), pp. 50–52.

46. See a note about the projected work in *Vecherniaia Moskva*, May 20, 1967.

47. See "Obnovlenie prozy," p. 125.

48. In an article of 1971 Kataev suggested that each work should be composed in a specific key and that the author's first task was to find the appropriate key. "Schast'e otkrytii," *Literaturnaia gazeta*, January 20, 1971.

49. This quotation is from Mandelshtam's essay "Slovo i kul'tura," *Sobranie sochinenii*, 11, pp. 264–69.

50. O. Mandel'shtam, "O prirode slova," *Sobranie sochinenii*, 11, p. 292.

51. It is interesting to compare these ideas with Olesha's many remarks about metaphors. Particularly important here are *Ni dnia bez strochki*, (*Not a Day Without a Line*) which undoubtedly influenced Kataev, and the story "Liubov'" ("Love"), which contains several examples of "the effect of presence." One of the materialized metaphors that so troubles the hero of that story is a wasp that becomes a tiger because the hero thinks of it as such. The fight with the wasp in *Kubik* may well owe something to Olesha's story. See Iu. Olesha, *"Liubov'," Izbrannoe* (Moscow, 1974), pp. 196–204.

52. Most critics of Kataev's works of the 1960s have admitted that the writing is of a high quality, but some have expressed unease at the private and aesthetic nature of his literary preoccupations. See V. Smirnova, "No zachem?," *Literaturnaia Rossiia*, July 11, 1969. In a curious way one is reminded of Mashbits-Verov's article of 1930 which also admitted Kataev's talent but judged him to be a harmful influence in Soviet literature because of his lack of commitment to the Soviet regime.

53. On this point see *My Diamond Crown*, passim; and V. Zhegis, "Goluboi fonar' vechnoi vesny," *Sovetskaia kul'tura*, August 4, 1978 (an interview with Kataev). Cited below as: Zhegis.

54. *Ni dnia bez strochki*, p. 11.

55. *Razbitaia zhizn'*, *Novyi mir*, 1972, no. 7, p. 8.

56. *Ni dnia bez strochki*, p. 40.

57. Ibid., p. 61.

58. *Razbitaia zhizn'*, *Novyi mir*, 1972, no. 7, p. 97.

59. On the similarity in point of view between Kataev and Ekaterina Gerasimovna see V. Kardin, "Siuzhet dlia nebol'shoi stat'i," *Voprosy literatury*, 1974, no. 5, pp. 72–93.

60. See Kataev's comments on "Violet" in Zhegis.

Chapter Seven

1. See Zhegis.

2. Ibid.

3. N. Mandelstam, p. 281.

4. *My Diamond Crown*, passim, especially p. 60.

Selected Bibliography

PRIMARY SOURCES

1. In Russian

Sobranie sochinenii v piati tomakh. Moscow: Khudozhestvennaia literatura, 1956–57.

Sobranie sochinenii v deviati tomakh. Moscow: Khudozhestvennaia literatura, 1968–72.

Almaznyi moi venets, Novyi mir, 1978 no. 6, pp. 3–146.

"Fialka," *Novyi mir,* 1973, no. 8, pp. 74–95.

Kladbishche v Skulianakh, Novyi mir, 1975, no. 10, pp. 30–179.

Razbitaia zhizn', ili Volshebnyi rog Oberona, Novyi mir, 1972, no. 7, pp. 3–139; no. 8, pp. 8–202.

2. In English

"The Golden Pen." In *Soviet Literature: An Anthology,* edited by G. Reavey and M. Slonim. London: Wishart, 1933.

"The Iron Ring." In *An Anthology of Russian Literature in the Soviet Period from Gorki to Pasternak,* edited by B. G. Guerney. New York: Vintage, 1960.

Embezzlers. Translated by C. Rougle. Ann Arbor: Ardis, 1975. In one volume with Yu. Olesha, *Envy.*

Squaring the Circle. In *Six Soviet Plays,* edited by E. Lyons. London: Lawrence and Wishart, 1935.

Time, Forward! Translated by C. Malamuth. Bloomington: Indiana University Press, 1976.

Lonely White Sail; or, Peace Is Where the Tempest Blows. Translated by C. Malamuth. London: Allen and Unwin, 1937; New York: Farrar and Rinehart, 1937.

The Wife. London: Hutchinson, 1946.

The Small Farm in the Steppe. Translated by Anna Bostock. London: Lawrence and Wishart, 1958.

The Holy Well. Translated by M. Hayward and H. Shukman. London: Harvill Press, 1967.

163

The Grass of Oblivion. Translated by R. Daglish. London: Macmillan, 1969.

A Mosaic of Life: or the Magic Horn of Oberon. Translated by M. Budburg and G. Latta. London: Angus and Robertson, 1976.

SECONDARY SOURCES

BRAININA, BERTA. *Valentin Kataev: ocherk tvorchestva.* Moscow: Khudozhestvennaia literatura, 1960. A short book serving as a general introduction to Kataev's work. Places too much emphasis on the works of the middle period and too little on the 1920s.

————. "O nekotorykh osobennostiakh stilia V. Kataeva." In *Sovetskaia khudozhestvennaia proza: Sbornik statei,* pp. 360–94. Moscow: Sovetskii pisatel', 1955. Worthwhile study which concentrates on Kataev's style.

BUBENNOV, MIKHAIL. "O novom romane Valentina Kataeva *Za vlast' Sovetov.*" *Pravda,* January 16–17, 1950. Long, critical review of *For the Power of the Soviets.* Of historical interest only.

DOBIN, EFIM. "Detal' i podrobnosti." *Literaturnaia gazeta,* December 15, 1959. Useful short study of Kataev's style.

DUDINTSEV, VLADIMIR. "Dve magii iskusstva." *Literaturnaia gazeta,* August 13, 1966. Notable review of *The Holy Well* by well-known novelist. Concludes that Kataev's technical brilliance goes hand in hand with a lack of humanity and moral fiber.

ERLIKH, ARON. "Oni rabotali v gazete." *Znamia,* 1958, no. 8, pp. 162–90. Memoir about Kataev and other famous contributors to *Gudok* and *Pravda.*

GREENE, MILITSA, ed. *Ustami Buninykh.* Vol. 1. Frankfurt/Main: Possev-Verlag, 1977. Diaries of Ivan and Vera Bunin give vivid picture of Odessa during Civil War. Contains several interesting references to Kataev.

IVANOVA, E. M. "Zamysel i stil' *Travy zabven'ia* V. Kataeva." *Metod i masterstvo* (Vologda), 1971, vyp. 3, pp. 210–27. One of several good articles about *The Grass of Oblivion* by a scholar who has specialized in Kataev's later works.

IVERNI, VIOLETTA. "Sotsrealizm s chelovecheskim litsom." *Kontinent,* 1976, no. 7, pp. 393–417. Interesting and provocative article by an emigré critic about Kataev's later works, especially "Violet."

KARDIN, V. "Siuzhet dlia nebol'shoi stat'i." *Voprosy literatury,* 1974, no. 5, pp. 72–93. Detailed study of "Violet" by a Soviet critic. Conclusions quite different from those of Iverni.

MANDELSTAM, NADEZHDA. *Hope against Hope.* London: Collins/Harvill, 1971. Contains fascinating and not unsympathetic portrait of Kataev in the 1930s.

MASHBITS-VEROV, IOSIF. "Na grani: Tvorchestvo Valentina Kataeva." *Na literaturnom postu,* 1930, no. 9, pp. 35–46, and no. 11, pp. 47–56. Important hostile article in RAPP journal which played a part in Kataev's "transformation" at the beginning of the 1930s. Contains a good survey of his work of the 1920s.

REILLY, ALAYNE. *America in Contemporary Soviet Literature,* pp. 117–71. New York: New York University Press, 1971. Detailed and quite useful study of one aspect of *The Holy Well.*

ROSSOLOVSKAIA, V. "Tvorchestvo Valentina Kataeva." *Molodaia gvardiia,* 1933, no. 6, pp. 125–32. Survey of early works by hostile critic.

SARNOV, BENEDIKT. "Ugl' pylaiushchii i kimval briatsaiushchii." *Voprosy literatury,* 1968, no. 1, pp. 21–49. The best of several first-class short studies of Kataev's work by this perceptive critic who reaches a conclusion similar to Dudintsev's. The same issue of the journal contains two other articles on Kataev of less interest.

SHKLOVSKII, VIKTOR. "O Valentine Kataeve." In *Staroe i novoe,* pp. 96–101. Moscow: Detskaia literatura, 1966. Reprint of early article by the famous critic. Contains some fine insights.

SIDEL'NIKOVA, TAT'IANA. *Valentin Kataev.* Moscow: Sovetskii pisatel', 1957. A useful book-length study of Kataev's career to the mid-1950s. Detailed discussion of the early works.

SKORINO, LIUDMILA. *Pisatel' i ego vremia.* Moscow: Sovetskii pisatel', 1965. Well-researched study of Kataev's career to 1964. Especially good on his life and times up to World War II. The best general study to date.

Index

DATE DUE
